Violence

Other Books of Related Interest

Teen Decisions Series
Alcohol
Pregnancy
Sex
Smoking

Opposing Viewpoints Series
Crime and Criminals
Domestic Violence
Gangs
Gun Control
Juvenile Crime
Sexual Violence
Teens at Risk
Violence

Current Controversies Series
Family Violence
Guns and Violence
Violence Against Women
Violence in the Media

Contemporary Issues Companions
Battered Women
Rape
School Violence
Violence Against Women
Youth Violence

At Issue Series
Date Rape
Domestic Violence
Guns and Crime
Rape on Campus
Violent Children

Violence

Bryan J. Grapes, *Book Editor*

David L. Bender, *Publisher*
Bruno Leone, *Executive Editor*
Bonnie Szumski, *Editorial Director*
Stuart B. Miller, *Managing Editor*
James D. Torr, *Series Editor*

Greenhaven Press Inc., San Diego, California

Library of Congress Cataloging-in-Publication Data

Violence / Bryan J. Grapes, book editor.
    p. cm. — (Teen decisions)
    Includes bibliographical references and index.
    ISBN 0-7377-0573-6 (pbk. : alk. paper) —
    ISBN 0-7377-0574-4 (lib. : alk. paper)
    1. Violence—United States. 2. Violence in adolescence—United States. 3. School violence—United States. 4. Dating violence—United States. I. Grapes, Bryan J. II. Series.

HN90.V5 V539 2001
303.6'9073—dc21
                                        00-058715
                                            CIP

Cover photo: © Michael Ventura/International Stock

©2001 by Greenhaven Press, Inc.
PO Box 289009, San Diego, CA 92198-9009

Printed in the U.S.A.

Contents

Foreword

The teen years are a time of transition from childhood to adulthood. By age 13, most teenagers have started the process of physical growth and sexual maturation that enables them to produce children of their own. In the United States and other industrialized nations, teens who have entered or completed puberty are still children in the eyes of the law. They remain the responsibility of their parents or guardians and are not expected to make major decisions themselves. In most of the United States, eighteen is the age of legal adulthood. However, in some states, the age of majority is nineteen, and some legal restrictions on adult activities, such as drinking alcohol, extend until age twenty-one.

This prolonged period between the onset of puberty and the achieving of legal adulthood is not just a matter of hormonal and physical change, but a learning process as well. Teens must learn to cope with influences outside the immediate family. For many teens, friends or peer groups become the basis for many of their opinions and actions. In addition, teens are influenced by TV shows, advertising, and music.

The *Teen Decisions* series aims at helping teens make responsible choices. Each book provides readers with thought-provoking advice and information from a variety of perspectives. Most of the articles in these anthologies were originally written for, and in many cases by, teens. Some of the essays focus on ethical and moral dilemmas, while others present pertinent legal and scientific information. Many of the articles tell personal stories about decisions teens have made and how their lives were affected.

One special feature of this series is the "Points of Contention," in which specially paired articles present directly opposing views on controversial topics. Additional features in each book include a listing of organizations to contact for more information, as well as a bibliography to aid readers interested in more information. The *Teen Decisions* series strives to include both trustworthy information and multiple opinions on topics important to teens, while respecting the role teens play in making their own choices.

Introduction

On April 20, 1999, eighteen-year-old Eric Harris and seventeen-year-old Dylan Klebold walked into Columbine High School in Littleton, Colorado, with an arsenal of high-powered firearms and explosives. Twelve classmates and one teacher were killed and twenty-three students were wounded before Harris and Klebold turned their guns on themselves.

Tragically, Columbine was just one of a wave of mass shootings that plagued American schools in the late 1990s. Between 1996 and 1999, nine mass shootings by teenagers at U.S. schools left a total of thirty-five students and teachers dead and seventy-six wounded. Although school violence represents only one aspect of the violence perpetrated by teenagers, these high-profile shootings have generated renewed concern about the problem of violence in American society. In their efforts to prevent school violence, parents, lawmakers, and teenagers have focused on trying to understand the causes of violent behavior in teenagers.

Teens and Guns

The relatively easy availability of guns in America is often cited as a contributing factor in the problem of teen violence. According to statistics gathered by Office of Juvenile Justice and Delinquency Prevention (OJJDP), the rate of gun-related juvenile homicide tripled between 1984 and 1994. OJJDP figures show that gun violence hits inner-city African American teenagers especially hard; gun-related homicide is the leading cause of death for black males between the ages of fifteen and nineteen. Many people believe that this rise in gun-related juvenile homicide is linked with the increasing availability of firearms. Gun control advocates note that the perpetrators of the school shootings were easily able to amass extensive arsenals of high-powered weapons. Writing of the massacre at Columbine, Jann S. Wenner, editor and publisher of *Rolling Stone,* explains that there is one irrefutably obvious lesson: "The nature and extent and devastation of the violence were directly and undeniably linked to the kind of weaponry that we have made widely available in America."

Statistics indicate that an alarming number of teenagers have taken a firearm to school and that most teens have excessively easy access to guns. According to Department of Education records, six thousand students were expelled during the 1996–97 school year for bringing firearms or explosives to school. In a 1999 survey of twelve- to twenty-four-year-olds, conducted by *Rolling Stone* and MTV, 84 percent of teens said they had easy access to a firearm. For most teens, getting a gun is as easy as getting a pack of cigarettes.

The reason most cited by teens for carrying a gun, particularly teenagers in tough inner-city neighborhoods, is protection. Many teens believe that carrying a gun—or any other weapon—will protect them from neighborhood drug dealers and gang members. However, most experts agree that this is not the case. Instead of defense, an armed teen will often use a gun to settle a personal dispute or as a way of dealing with re-venge, anger, and hurt. According to James Alan Fox, when guns and volatile tempers are mixed, fatal shootings typically ensue. Fox, the dean of the College of Criminal Justice at Northeastern University, argues that teenagers with guns are dangerous because they are too young to have complete con-trol over their impulses and emotions. Fox believes that teens are unable to fully comprehend the tragic consequences of pulling the trigger. Consequently, teens "are more willing to pull the trigger over trivial matters—a leather jacket, a pair of sneakers, a challenging remark, or no reason at all."

Not everyone, however, believes that the availability of guns is responsible for deadly outbursts like the one perpetrated by Eric Harris and Dylan Klebold. Dustin Thurman, a Columbine senior when Harris and Klebold went on their rampage, believes that teen violence has more to do with an absence of morals than with the availability of guns. In an April 30, 1999, interview conducted by the *New York Times*, Thurman points out that he, like many other Littleton residents, owns a number of firearms: "I could run around and start shooting people easily. But it's morals. You just know right from wrong."

Violent Pop Culture

The massacre at Columbine also renewed the debate surrounding America's violent popular culture and the influence it has on young people's behavior. You have no doubt read that Eric Harris and Dylan Klebold were avid fans of violent video games like *Doom* and *Quake,* and how Michael Carneal, the boy responsible for the December 1997 shooting at Heath High School in West Paducah, Kentucky, that left three of his classmates dead, might have been inspired to open fire on his classmates by a scene in the movie *The Basketball Diaries.* Many psychological experts and media critics contend that repeated exposure to violent images and song lyrics desensitizes teenagers to the pain and suffering caused by real violence. "Almost no one, except for a few blinded by financial stakes, thinks that the popular culture is not having a coarsening effect on our kids. The evidence, empirical and anecdotal, is overwhelming," charges former education secretary William J. Bennett.

Other experts feel that violent video games, television shows, movies, and music send the message that violence is an acceptable way to solve your problems. In her testimony before the U.S. House of Representatives Subcommittee on Early Childhood, Youth, and Families, author and media expert Joanne Cantor concedes that the school shootings were the "result of many unhealthy influences working together." However, Cantor feels that the link between media violence and juvenile violence is too obvious to ignore:

> When a child resorts to gunfire to correct what he sees as an injustice, is it unreasonable to think that repeated exposure to violent incidents on television—25 percent of which involve guns—might have provided encouragement to act that way? In many of these well-publicized incidents, the young perpetrators seemed surprised at the severity of the consequences to themselves and their victims. Maybe the fact that violence on television usually underplays violence's negative effects has something to do with this.

Correlations and Causality

Yet many researchers have pointed out that while a correlation may exist between teens' exposure to violent images and aggressive behavior, there is no proof that exposure to violent media actually *causes* violent behavior. According to Jonathan Freedman, a professor of psychology at the University of Toronto, it could be just as reasonably argued that viewing violent television shows, or playing violent video games is caused by a teen's preexisting tendency to be aggressive.

> Correlations do not prove causality. Boys watch more TV football than girls, and they play more football than girls, but no one, as far as I know, believes that television is what makes boys more interested in football. Probably personality characteristics that make children more aggressive also make them prefer violent television programs.

Teens themselves also downplay the influence that violent pop culture has on their behavior. In an interview with the *New York Times,* Meg Hains, a seventeen-year-old junior at Columbine at the time of the shootings, argues that games like *Doom* are actually therapeutic because they provide a harmless way to vent anger.

> I've played the game *Doom* that they're saying Dylan and Eric

constantly played. And I don't think [the reason they killed thirteen people] was that game. I'd go to school and there were people that would so royally piss me off, and I'd just go home and I'd sit on that game for hours, just taking out my stress on it. And the next day I'd be perfectly fine.

That's the way I get rid of my stress, instead of going out and really killing people.

The Cruel Social Hierarchy at School

Though the majority of the debate on the causes of teen violence has centered on guns and violent pop culture, the carnage at Littleton and other schools has shed light on another aspect of teen life that seldom receives attention—bullying. According to the National School Safety Center, bullying is "the most enduring and underrated problem in American schools." As the investigators in the Columbine shooting discovered, bullying is often an underlying cause of violent outbursts by teens. It is widely acknowledged that Eric Harris and Dylan Klebold were favorite targets for verbal and physical harassment by Columbine's athletes. Harris and Klebold, along with others of outcast status at Columbine, were regularly slammed into lockers and called "faggots." Luke Woodham, the boy responsible for the October 1997 shooting in Pearl, Mississippi, that left two classmates dead and seven wounded, was also regularly harassed by the popular students at his school. Many of the other perpetrators of school shootings had similar experiences. Some observers speculate that Harris, Klebold, Woodham, and the others were pushed over the edge by years of torment. Both Woodham and Harris left notes detailing the reasons behind their rampages. Woodham wrote: "I am not insane. I am angry. I killed because people like me are mistreated every day. I did this to show society, 'Push us and we will push back.'"

In his suicide note, Harris explicitly states that his actions were the not the result of violent pop culture, but of years of ostracism and ridicule at the hands of his classmates. Harris also blames Littleton's parents and teachers for teaching Columbine's teens to not accept what is different and for making such ridicule possible.

Empathy for the Killers

Odd as it may seem, there was no shortage of empathy for the Columbine gunmen once details of daily school life in Littleton were released. "Kids That Kill," a piece written by Jon Katz for *Slashdot.org* that detailed the tortured lives of outsiders in school, generated a flood of email responses to the website from people who had endured similar abuse. Adults and teens all over the country wrote in to newspapers and websites to relate horrific tales of bullying and ostracism. In an interview with Susan Greene of the *Denver Post,* an anonymous member of the Trenchcoat Mafia (the group of Columbine outcasts with whom Harris and Klebold were loosely affiliated) described how unpopular students were regularly sideswiped by jocks in speeding cars and verbally and physically terrorized on a daily basis. "Pure hell," is how he described his life at Columbine. "I can understand why they wanted to destroy their school and kill their classmates, because when I was that age, I felt the same way towards my school and classmates. Much like Eric and Dylan, I was an object of constant ridicule from about fifth grade until my high school graduation. . . . I still carry the scars from public education," writes William Malverson, a computer programmer who posted the details of his years in school on the internet.

While no one condoned the actions of Eric Harris and Dylan Klebold, many who endured similar abuse understood why they finally snapped. Dan Savage, a syndicated sex columnist, had this to say about the Columbine massacre:

> This is the lesson that's not being learned. There are social dynamics in high schools that are every bit as murderous as what these kids did, except they're stretched out over years and years. I'd be interested to know how many ostracized kids there have committed suicide over time.

They kept saying on the news, "How could this happen, in a place where children feel safe?" Did you go to high school in this country? Even to some extent the kids who engage in the worst social ostracism and sadism are also acting out of their insecurity and the lack of physical safety. Every day I was in school it was like a fucking nightmare. I'm surprised it didn't happen then—I'm surprised I didn't do it.

"Someone Had to Notice That Something Was Wrong"

Many observers feel that violent episodes like the Columbine massacre will continue until educators, parents, and teens take a strong stance against all forms of harassment. David Yarovesky, a student and self-described social outcast at Calabasas High School in Los Angeles, hopes that massacres like Littleton will draw attention to the often-cruel social hierarchy of school. While he does not condone the actions of the shooters, Yarovesky does sympathize with ostracized students like them. "I feel that [the Columbine massacre] had to happen," Yarovesky said. "Someone had to notice that something was wrong at school."

Likewise, Mike H., a high school student from Westford, Massachusetts, hopes that the shootings in Pearl, West Paducah, Littleton, and other towns will inspire teens to treat their fellow students with more respect. "Can you truly say you have never made fun of anyone?" he asks in a column posted on TeenInk.com. "I know I can't." Mike expresses remorse for partaking in the kind of harassment that may have driven teens like Woodham, Carneal, Harris, and Klebold over the edge, and he ends his column with a bit of advice: "I can only suggest that everyone think about how they treat others in order to try to prevent a catastrophe like this from happening again. I know I will."

Exploring the Issues of Teen Violence

Though media coverage of the string of school shootings during the late 1990s would seem to indicate otherwise, the chances of a Columbine-like massacre occurring at your school are very slim. Most studies indicate that violence in schools has actually decreased. According to a 1998 report by the U.S. Departments of Justice and Education, you have a greater chance of being struck by lightning than getting murdered on school grounds, and statistics gathered by writers Jerry Adler and Karen Springen in the May 3, 1999, edition of *Newsweek* indicate that a high school senior is two hundred times as likely to be admitted to Harvard as to be killed in his or her school. Most incidents of teen violence manifest themselves in bullying, fistfights, and relationship violence, not lethal schoolyard shootings. But while these types of violence are less physically dangerous, they are an alarmingly commonplace part of many teens' lives. The threat that violence poses to you, and how you can avoid it, are the issues explored in *Teen Decisions: Violence*. In Chapter One, School Violence, the authors examine the safety of today's schools, the social climate in the classroom, and whether or not zero-tolerance policies have a pronounced impact on school violence. Chapter Two, Teens and Guns, examines the impact that firearms have on teen violence, as well as the views of teens who have experience gun-related violence. Chapter Three, Violence in Relationships, offers the perspectives of teens, and friends of teens who were involved in abusive relationships. Chapter Four, Avoiding Violence, offers constructive ways to vent anger and aggression, how to avoid violent confrontations, and how to deal with bullies. It is hoped that *Teen Decisions: Violence* will provide you with the information you need to get through your teen years safely.

Chapter 1

School Violence

Should You Worry About School Violence?

KidsHealth.org

Though the April 1999 school massacre at Columbine High School in Littleton, Colorado, may make you think otherwise, the chances of a mass shooting occurring at your school are very low. According to recent statistics, school is the safest place you can be. Your school is probably safer than your own home. However, it is important to be watchful of students who display the warning signs of violent behavior, such as playing with weapons, making threats to classmates, and becoming preoccupied with violent entertainment. If a classmate displays these traits, you should report it to a teacher right away. KidsHealth.org is one of the largest sights on the Internet providing doctor-approved health information about children and teens.

Not too long ago, you couldn't even turn on the TV or pick up a newspaper without hearing about the shootings at Columbine High School in Littleton, Colorado. Even if you weren't paying a lot of attention to the media, all the talk at the family dinner table or at the mall with your friends could give you the feeling that schools are not safe places to be.

Following an incident as devastating as the one at Columbine, it's a good idea to step back and take a bigger look at things. When we're caught up in the emotions of the story and our own fears, it's easy to lose sight of what the truth really is. It's also easy to feel overwhelmed and forget there are things you can do in your own school to help.

A Wider View

If we're going to take a look at school violence, it's important to have a clear sense of what violence actually means. Even though incidents like the one in Colorado tend to get all the attention, if you've ever been ruthlessly teased at school, laughed at, shoved around, or bullied, you know there's more to violence in school than mass killings.

A good definition of school violence might be this: violence is a person's or group's behavior or language that causes another person to become hurt, physically or psychologically. That can include assaults (either physical fights or attacks with guns or other objects), bullying, extreme teasing, or physical or emotional intimidation (taunting or name calling, for example). Violence can be directed against students, staff, or teachers and can occur at any time of the day or night.

How Safe Is My School?

Maybe your school has metal detectors or security guards at the front doors, but this isn't always a sign that your school isn't safe. It may seem like a pain to have to wait in line just to get into the building, but it's all part of what your school is doing to keep you safe.

The truth is, there's very little likelihood that something like what happened at Columbine will happen in your school.

According to Bob Chase, president of the National Education Association (NEA), school is actually the safest place you can be—it's safer than being at the mall, on the street, or even inside your home. The Centers for Disease Control and Prevention (CDC) agrees, reporting that the number of school-associated violent deaths has been decreasing since the 1992 to 1993 school year.

Reprinted by permission of Jimmy Margulies.

Although the number of events involving more than one victim has been on the rise (averaging five between 1995 and 1998), the U.S. Department of Education says that 43% of the schools in the country had no crime at all. When crimes are committed, theft and vandalism (not crimes against people) are the leading types.

Even though the statistics should reassure you that school is the safest place for you to be, it can be hard to ignore the media reports and any fears you may have. School violence isn't easy to understand.

Who's to Blame?

That's the question that baffles everyone. In the wake of a tragedy like the one in Colorado, almost everyone feels powerless. It's human nature to want to find out why, but the truth is, the answers aren't simple.

There is no single reason why some people become violent. Sometimes, they're just copying behavior they've seen at home, on the streets, or in video games, movies, or television shows. Sometimes, they've been the victims of teasing who have hit a limit and feel like they would do anything to make it stop.

> There's more to violence in school than mass killing.

Peer pressure also can lead some teens to violence. If your friends are daring or pushing you to act, it takes a lot of guts to stand up to them and refuse to do what they're trying to make you do—whether it's spray painting a wall or getting into a fight with someone who's different than you.

Guys seem to be particularly prone to acting out their feelings in a violent way.

Alcohol and drugs can reduce your inhibitions, which means you might find yourself saying and doing things you never would if you were sober.

Experts all seem to agree that the availability of guns or other weapons makes it even easier for some people to strike out against the things or people they don't like.

What If I Get Scared?

If you start feeling unsafe at school, the first thing you need to do is find an adult to talk to. That person could be your teacher, your parent, a school counselor, or someone in your church or synagogue.

Talking is something that can be hard to do. Maybe you've been threatened if you do speak up. Or you're scared you won't be believed. What if the other kids find out? Will they tease you? Would they try to retaliate?

None of that matters, really. You and an adult you trust can talk everything through and come up with a solution that is good for your particular circumstances. Besides, not talking about the problem won't make it go away.

It's also really important to say something if you notice one of your classmates talking or acting differently. People who are on the verge of violence usually display warning signs. The talk you have with a teacher or other adult could mean the difference between life and death. Things to look

Mass Shootings in American Schools Since 1996

- *February 2, 1996* Barry Loukaitis killed two students and one teacher and wounded one student at his school in Moses Lake, Washington.
- *February 19, 1997* Evan Ramsey shot and killed one teacher and one classmate in his Bethel, Alaska, high school.
- *October 1, 1997* Luke Woodham killed two classmates and wounded seven others at his high school in Pearl, Mississippi.
- *December 1, 1997* Michael Carneal shot and killed three students and wounded five others at Heath High School in West Paducah, Kentucky.
- *March 24, 1998* Mitchell Johnson and Andrew Golden killed four students and one teacher and wounded ten others at Westside Middle School in Jonesboro, Arkansas.
- *April 24, 1998* Andrew Wurst opened fire at a school dance in Edinboro, Pennsylvania, killing one teacher and wounding two classmates.
- *May 21, 1998* Kipland Kinkel shot and killed two students and wounded twenty-two others at Thurston High School in Springfield, Oregon.
- *April 20, 1999* Eric Harris and Dylan Klebold killed twelve classmates and one teacher and wounded twenty-three others before turning their guns on themselves at Columbine High School in Littleton, Colorado.
- *May 20, 1999* T.J. Solomon opened fire in a hallway at Heritage High School in Conyers, Georgia, wounding six.

out for in other students include:
- playing with weapons of any kind
- repeatedly watching violent movies or playing violent games
- bullying or threatening other people
- cruelty to pets or other animals

"We were always taught not to tattle," says Pamela Riley, executive director of the Center for Prevention of School Violence. "We still should not indiscriminately talk about other people, but if we think there might be a dangerous situation, it's important to let a responsible adult know about it."

Getting Involved

Why not become actively involved in making your school an even safer place to be?

You could set up an anonymous hot line. That way, students in your school would have a way to share their concerns about someone who may become violent without worrying about what might happen if they are seen reporting the person's behavior.

Even though the statistics should reassure you that school is the safest place for you to be, it can be hard to ignore the media reports and any fears you may have.

Some schools hold stop-the-violence rallies before sports events or assemblies. Another idea would be to plan fight-free days, where students make a day-long commitment to avoiding conflict. Teachers could help you set up a student mediation panel, allowing students to become actively involved in problem solving.

Maybe you could even help your school set up a page on the school's Web site to address concerns about school violence. Concerned students could email their thoughts—in private—to a guidance counselor or teacher through the site.

Another alternative might be to join an existing school or

community club or organization that's dedicated to helping teens stay safe. Ask your teacher or guidance counselor for ideas, or check out your local volunteer opportunities.

The important thing to remember is that school is just the about the safest place for you to be, but if you ever feel like it's not, there will always be someone you can talk to about it.

How to Feel Safe at School

Debi Martin-Morris

According to freelance writer Debi Martin-Morris, several highly publicized mass shootings in American schools have left many high school students worried about school safety. Some research indicates that as many 36 percent of students believe that kids in their school were capable of committing a massacre like the April 1999 shooting at Columbine High School in Littleton, Colorado. However, Morris explains, there are many ways for students to prevent violence at their schools. Talking about your fear is the first step toward creating a safer atmosphere at school. Peer mediation and teen counseling centers are other effective methods in creating a safe school environment.

Why Lauren?
Why did this have to happen?
What did she ever do in her life to deserve such a fate?
Why not me?
Rachel Goodwin wrote these words on the final day of school, before she graduated from Columbine High School in May 1999 in the aftermath of what has been called the worst school shoot-

Reprinted from "After Columbine: How to Feel Safe at School Again," by Debi Martin-Morris, *Teen*, October 1999. Reprinted with permission from *Teen*.

ing in U.S. history. One of the 12 students killed in the Littleton, Colorado, school was 18-year-old Lauren Townsend, volleyball captain, valedictorian candidate and Rachel's best friend.

"I still cry over Lauren," Rachel said in June 1999. "To me, Lauren was a teammate, a best friend, a future roommate, cut down before she could even experience life."

Rachel lost a friend, and with each school shooting all teens lost something precious: the feeling that "it can't happen here," that school is a safe place where a classmate won't suddenly pull out a gun and start shooting. But Rachel knows she has to find ways to help herself heal. So she started writing her feelings down as an assignment in psychology class.

"At first I was like, oh no, I don't want to do this, I don't want to feel all this," she said. "I thought it would be really painful, but it all just came out. It actually felt good to write it down. I realized that it's better to let the feelings out than hold it all in."

On the Road to Recovery

There is no single way to grieve, and the stages—anger, denial, depression and acceptance—occur randomly. "At times you may feel different emotions," says Stacy Kalamaros Skalski, Ph.D., a professor of school psychology at the University of Colorado at Denver. Most people don't experience grief the same way, either: "You might expect a friend to be feeling what you are, when in reality the friend is dealing with his or her grief in a completely different way."

Many Columbine students reacted to the tragedy with shock and disbelief, says Jo Anne Doherty of the Jefferson Center for Mental Health, who led the local psychological crisis-response effort after the shooting. "A lot of these kids turned inward and had a hard time sleeping or concentrating. They were edgy and startled easily by noises," she says.

Doherty says the Columbine teens were encouraged to talk or express their feelings however they could. "Some of them paint.

Some write. Dumping it out, any way you can, that's what helps," she says, emphasizing that holding feelings in can lead to serious depression.

Talking about what happened—to friends, her parents and God—helped Missy Jenkins, who was shot and paralyzed from the chest down in the December 1, 1997, shooting at Heath High School in West Paducah, Kentucky. "Sometimes I want to talk about it constantly," says Missy, who went to her prom last May in a wheelchair. "The more I talk, the more normal I feel—I can concentrate more on the present. I didn't think it would ever go away. But I don't think about it now as much as I used to."

For kids who've been through school shootings, a bad memory can be triggered any time. Not surprisingly, to Crystal Amanda Barnes, who was wounded at Westside Middle School in Jonesboro, Arkansas, on March 24, 1998, the tragedy in Littleton hit close to home. The day of the Columbine shooting, she says, "I went home from school early—I was so scared. I just wanted to go home and be safe."

> For kids who've been through school shootings, a bad memory can be triggered at any time.

Richard Storbeck says that facing his fears head-on helped him deal. In the fall of 1998 he returned to Thurston High in Springfield, Oregon, after the May 1998 shooting there. "My parents," says Richard, "who I thought were the stupidest people in the world, helped me. They told me, 'You can't live in fear—face that fear.'" Richard, a French horn player, says music and talking to his friends also helped him handle his anxiety. "Sometimes I feel scared and I have to let it out," he says. "Mostly I try to forget about it. It's a balancing act, but you just can't let it control your life."

The Statistics: You Feel Unsafe

Surveys show that students are aware of the problems in their schools, and that they recognize some simple remedies: more talking and better understanding. But the statistics are scary. One poll taken before the Columbine tragedy reported that 47 percent of students in grades 7 through 12 said it was easy for them to get a gun. In another poll, 36 percent of teens ages 13 to 17 said there were kids in their schools who were capable of that type of violence. Forty percent of the students rated poor peer relations as the worst cause of violence. Close to one fourth of the students ranked personal problems as second, and only a small number of students said violence was caused by parents, family or warning signs that were ignored.

> Metal detectors and beefed-up school security are not effective without other programs that directly involve and empower students.

When asked how to reduce the likelihood of a crisis like Littleton at their schools, nearly a quarter of the teens said better security, counseling, communication and tolerance would help.

Another study, "Reducing Fear in the Schools," released after the Jonesboro shooting, showed that teasing, insults and the pressure to fit in fuel outbreaks of violent behavior. Savvy students also said that metal detectors and beefed-up school security are not effective without other programs that directly involve and empower students.

What You Can Do

"Kids can do a lot to prevent school violence," says Skalski. "The more they're involved, the safer schools will be." One of the most successful student-driven approaches to encouraging tolerance is conflict resolution using peer mediators.

Fourteen-year-old Amy Ortiz became a peer mediator when she was 12. At Alameda Middle School in Santa Fe, New Mexico, the mediators are students who are trained to resolve feuds. Mediation referral slips are located around the school, and referrals are confidential. When there's a problem, the people involved sit down, and a peer mediator tries to get them to communicate their differences and talk about solutions. After they reach an agreement, they put it in writing for future reference. "Conflict resolution teaches you to see other people's viewpoints without making judgments," Amy says.

She adds that conflicts are often caused by misunderstandings started by rumors, or unresolved family issues students take out on each other. "Knowing that there is a constructive way to take care of a problem makes me feel safer at school," she says.

For Amy, it's simple: If everybody could learn to use problem solving in their daily lives instead of jumping to conclusions and getting angry, "we could have a whole new world!"

Signs of Hope

Some students are taking action by reaching out to give comfort and support. Columbine students Keira O'Dell and Julie McGinley helped start a teen drop-in counseling center in Littleton called S.H.O.U.T.S., Students Helping Others to Unite Together Socially.

Another group of Columbine students began their mission when they learned about the gunfire at Heritage High in Conyers, Georgia. "We were in English class when we heard about the shooting," says Heather Lietz, "and one of the girls said, 'Let's go there.' Then we got serious. We talked about how everybody had given us so much, we should give back. We felt we were the only people who could say to those kids, 'We know how you feel, and you are not alone.'"

In June 1999, still grieving from their own tragedy, Heather, four schoolmates and a teacher went to Conyers. "We told the kids there that life does go on," says Heather. "You will survive. You may see things in your head, and loud noises will bug you. You've got to talk about it. Everything happens so fast that nobody knows how to react. We told them the feelings will come. You just have to cry."

The group also issued a hopeful press statement: "The message we want to send is for the nation to open its eyes, ears and hearts to the youth of America. We hope to set in motion a change in American society for the better. Our goals are to improve communication . . . to take responsibility for the problems in our lives and not blame others. Blame often leads to hate, and hate too often leads to violence. To stop the violence, we need to stop the hate."

Sometimes It's Not Easy to Walk Away

Zainab Muhammad

Sometimes it's not possible to walk away from a confrontation at school, writes Zainab Muhammad, especially if your school is in a tough Brooklyn, New York, neighborhood like hers. Though she wishes it were otherwise, Muhammad describes the social situation at her school as a food chain—the strong survive and the weak get eaten. In this atmosphere, walking away from a challenge could mark someone as a victim or target. Muhammad writes that she responds with words if possible, however, if someone hits her she would not hesitate to hit back.

It was near the end of the day and there were so many students hanging around my school, it was chaos in the hallway.

"Yo, duke, you just stepped on my foot," said Jason. Although he knew it was a small incident, he was standing with his friends and he was not about to get "sonned" in front of them.

"Shut the f-ck up," said Malike, one of the school thugs. Everyday he is either in, or involved in, a fight.

Even though Jason and his friends knew Malike's reputation, they wanted to see a fight.

"Yo, what'd you say," said Jason's friends.

"I ain't say nothing," said Malike.

"Yo, that my word, I should smack that sh-t out of you," said Jason.

I've Put Up My Guard

By this time, everyone had stopped to look at what was going on.

As Malike went to turn around, Jason snatched off his do-rag. This got Malike even angrier.

He turned around and punched Jason in his mouth. This caused a major fight between Jason, Malike, his friends and even people who had nothing to do with it.

This is just one example of the kinds of things that happen in my school on a regular basis.

I go to Transit Tech High School in East New York, Brooklyn. When I came to this school two years ago, I was quiet and wholesome. Actually, I still am.

But after seeing so many fights, in some ways I've become a product of my environment. I've put up my guard, become more protective, and at times, even more aggressive.

Don't Make Me an Easy Target

Now don't get me wrong, I am a very friendly person who can get along with just about anybody. But if someone insults me, I'll respond with an insult. In the past, I would have just ignored it.

And before I got to my school, if I saw someone get jumped in the street, I would think about that all day. I would be angry to see someone get hurt that way.

But if I saw the same thing happen now, sure, I would care, but I would put it behind me, or I would find some way to justify it, like saying, "She should have kept her mouth shut," or, "It's his fault."

Some people might say that this attitude is negative. But I say that my attitude comes with good reason, because if I didn't adapt to my school, I would have become an easy target.

I think that I and all my peers would love to be in an environment where there is no problem with fighting or gaining respect.

But anyone who goes to a tough New York high school knows that is unrealistic. Unfortunately, for people who try to follow the rules, school becomes even harder.

So even though I'm still nice most of the time, until my school becomes safer, I'm going to look out for myself.

Around My School: Drug Spots and Barren Lots

Before you judge me, let me tell you a little bit more about my school and you can decide for yourself what I should do.

My school has about 1,000 students. Most of the people in my school live in East New York, Brownsville and Bed-Stuy. The area around the school has a pretty bad reputation for drug dealing and a lot of crime.

It's desolate and very run down, and it's not unusual to see a whole block empty except for the occasional drug spots and barren lots.

I live in South Jamaica, Queens. It's a very quiet, middle-class community. So when I first got to my school I was surprised by the difference.

There were certain things that I saw in school that I had never seen before, like gangs. Sure, there were plenty of "gangs" in my old school, but mainly they were just talk.

I never saw a gang conflict or even understood the true meaning of a gang until I came to my new school.

Now it's not unusual to see someone getting robbed for their Avirex [a popular jacket] or confronted because they have on the wrong colors.

Violence Finds Its Way into Our Hallways

In my old school, sometimes we would sit around and talk about a fistfight that we had heard about or might have seen. But when

I came to my new school, I was very surprised to hear about how often people talked about seeing someone get shot in the stomach or head.

It was not just the fact that they could sit around and talk about shootings, it was also their lackadaisical attitude about it. They talked about it as if it was something that happened every day.

Of course, there weren't any shootings going on in the school. Most of the violence that they talked about happened in their neighborhoods.

Yet it seemed as if it still found its way into our hallways, classrooms and our learning environment in general.

Now don't get me wrong. For the most part, I do feel safe in my school. I've been there a while, and I've established myself. Besides, there's plenty of security, and we even have police.

> When I came to my new school, I was very surprised to hear how often people talked about seeing someone get shot in the stomach or head.

But that sense of security had to grow on me. In the beginning, I wasn't used to the way people in my school acted, and I definitely did not feel comfortable.

Freshman Fears

As a freshman, I would watch fights in my math class almost every day. The first fight I saw was on the second day of school.

A boy smacked a girl because she was sucking her finger and he thought that she was mimicking him. I was surprised, but I figured it was the first few days of school and they were just getting used to each other.

But soon after, I noticed that fights were an everyday thing in that class and I began to feel afraid.

I was not afraid that I would get beat up. I was really afraid that fights were going to be the only thing that I would see in my four years of high school and that my grades would be affected.

Which they were. After about three weeks of fighting, my math teacher got fed up and stopped teaching.

He said he would only give private lessons to the students who he felt wanted to learn. I was not one of those students.

I had only one other class besides math where there was so much fighting, but seeing it on a regular basis affected my school work overall.

After a few months, seeing fights became so normal to me that one time, when two boys were having a fistfight right where I was sitting, I just continued to sit in my seat as they fought on my desk.

My grades were pretty bad at that point, so breaking up the fight so I could resume with my schoolwork didn't seem logical. It is as if I became desensitized to it.

My New Mission: Gain Respect, Not Friends

After a while, I began to change the way I behaved, too.

When I first got to my school, I tried to be nice to everyone, even the ones I hated. But then I started to notice that people were either walking all over me or just using me.

So I decided that my mission was not to gain friends but to gain respect from my classmates. This toughened me up.

And seeing all those fights, I developed an attitude that I was bound to have a fight no matter what I did to avoid it.

So as quiet as I was, I always had some sort of plan about what I would do if anyone started trouble with me.

My mother grew up in the same neighborhood where I go to school, so she had more of an idea what the area would be like before I got there.

She taught me that if someone hits you, you should hit them back. If I ever got into a fight in school and I let the person hit me and I did not hit them back, I would get into trouble.

I don't think that my mother taught me this because she wanted me to be a violent, out-of-control person. I think she taught me that because she did not want me to be "soft."

When my mother talked to me about the fights that she had when she was younger, she did not glorify her fights, but her experiences helped me figure out how I would handle tough situations.

Bonding with My Bully

One of the first times I stood up for myself was in the 9th grade. This boy would always "start" with me.

One day when we were in biology class he told me to shut up and sit down. That was small compared to the other things he used to say, but it still made me very angry.

I decided I was not going to take any more, so we got into a argument in the hallway. I stopped being the little quiet person that I had been and I told him all the things I had wanted to tell him for a long time.

At the time, I should have been afraid, but I was not. Afterwards I was very surprised.

I was surprised that I had finally stood up for myself. And I was surprised that he did not punch me in my mouth.

I had never gotten into a fight before and I really didn't argue with people in school, so to me that fight was a big deal.

A few days later I noticed a difference in my classmate. When I walked into my class, the boy said hi to me (which is something that he had never done), and that gave me total self-confidence.

As the year went on, we started to become closer, and I realized that, although he was a bully, he wasn't all bad.

I also realized that I never would have been able to learn that if I had remained quiet and secluded, because then he would have continued to pick on me. That's just the way some people in my school are.

If I wanted to be friends with them, first I would have to learn to stand up to them.

Stand Up for Yourself or Be Socially Destroyed

Everyone says that violence is bad. Many people might say that if someone wants to fight you, walking away is the solution.

But if you do that in my school, you stand a big chance of being socially destroyed. If word gets around school that you backed out of a fight, most likely, people will label you a herb for the entire school term.

Let me give you just one example. There was a boy named Jack who I had classes with this year.

He would sit around with me and a few other classmates and tell us about the fights he had been in and what he would do if anyone in the school ever "stepped" to him.

One day, another boy, Chris, confronted him.

Chris cracked jokes on his mother, his clothes and a few other things, which is usually grounds for fighting. But Jack ignored him, and everyone laughed at him.

> My school is like a food chain. The strongest survive. The weakest get eaten up.

We laughed not because it was funny, but because Jack was not a "tough guy" anymore. His image was ruined.

Eventually the story got around school and people started to call Jack a scrub and some other not nice stuff.

A few days later, Jack got robbed by two freshmen in the train station. I'd say the two incidents were related.

Unfortunately, that's not surprising. My school is like a food chain. The strongest survive. The weakest get eaten up.

I'd love to go to a school where that wasn't true.

But I also think it's pointless to preach to each one of us about walking away unless everyone's willing to do it.

Until that happens, I'm going to stand up for myself, even if that means taking on a fight.

Point of Contention: Are Zero-Tolerance Laws Effective in Creating Safe Schools?

In the wake of several highly publicized mass shootings at American schools between 1996 and 1999, many school boards instituted drastic security measures in the hopes of preventing a catastrophic violent outburst by one of their students. Metal detectors, surveillance cameras, drug-sniffing dogs, armed guards, random searches and seizures of students' lockers and property, and a zero-tolerance policy for breaking the rules have become commonplace in schools across America. While some feel that these measures are necessary and effective in maintaining a safe atmosphere in school, others contend that these measures are oppressive and violate students' constitutional rights. The *New Republic* is a conservative journal of politics and the arts. Nadine Strossen is president of the American Civil Liberties Union (ACLU).

Zero-Tolerance Laws Are Making Schools Safer

New Republic

"The so-called zero-tolerance policy is without mercy and without sensitivity," the Reverend Jesse Jackson declared in November 1999, protesting the Decatur, Illinois, school board's decision to expel six students for inciting a melee at a football game. Jackson is not alone in his view. The American Civil Liberties Union, civil rights leaders, and others on the left also want zero-tolerance laws abolished. Illinois Representative Bobby Rush is calling for congressional hearings on their legality; he's even asked U.S. Attorney General Janet Reno for an investigation.

And it's true that zero-tolerance laws are sometimes flawed in design or execution. It's also true that they effectively combat perhaps the greatest crisis in public education today: the crisis of violence. To call them inherently racist is to imply that a strictly disciplined school, a school where students learn without fear, serves only the interests of whites. And it is that proposition, it seems to us, that represents racism of the most debilitating kind.

In fact, zero tolerance has a liberal pedigree; it was originally the brainchild of the late Albert Shanker's American Federation of Teachers (AFT). In Cincinnati in 1990, the AFT discovered that local teachers were spending enormous amounts of time dealing with drugs, guns, assaults, and brawls. "In basically half the classrooms in the city, the teachers couldn't teach effectively," said Tom Mooney, vice president of the union. In 1991, Cincinnati responded by establishing automatic penalties for students who commit violent acts or are caught with drugs, alcohol, or weapons. Texas followed suit two years later. In 1994, Congress required states to pass zero-tolerance laws or forfeit federal money.

Zero Tolerance Works
Since then, counties and cities have extended the list of zero-tolerance violations. And while these statutes have led to occasional excesses—such as the eighth-grade honors student in Georgia suspended for bringing his French

teacher a bottle of vintage wine as a Christmas present—in most cases the laws are working. In Texas, a survey found that from 1993 to 1998, the percentage of teachers who viewed assaults on students as a "significant problem" dropped from 53 to 31. In Baltimore, where schools had been rife with violence, an aggressive zero-tolerance law adopted last spring has produced a 30 percent drop in student assaults on other students and a 50 percent decrease in student assaults on teachers and other staff.

> [Zero-tolerance laws] effectively combat perhaps the greatest crisis in public education today: the crisis of school violence.

But, for the critics, the evidence that zero tolerance makes schools safer is beside the point. The victims of school violence are not the ones over whom they lose sleep. What, they ask, do such laws do for the students who get suspended or expelled? Ruth Zweifler, executive director of the Michigan Student Advocacy Center, says that her state's zero-tolerance law "erodes our commitment to public education. Underneath it is the message that we no longer believe we need to educate all children." No; the message is that we will not, in the name of educating all children, force the vast majority to live under conditions that make education impossible. Shanker, a holdover from an age of grittier, less therapeutic liberalism, understood this. "Some people," he said in 1995, "think of schools as sort of custodial institutions. . . . Or they think the school's job is socialization. . . . The central role of the schools . . . is academic achievement. We have to be tough because basically we are defending the right of children to an education."

Behind the other objections, of course, lies one central one: that zero-tolerance laws are racist. The NAACP cites statistics showing that black students are more likely than white students to be suspended or expelled. To be sure, when a particular school singles out blacks and coddles whites, school boards should conduct a careful review. But, in most cases, the racial disparity in expulsions is smaller than the racial disparity in arrests for violent crimes. That African American students may be statistically more likely than other students to commit violent acts is a grave problem that demands serious government attention to the conditions under which African American children grow up. But to use that disparity as a reason to tolerate acts of violence is to condemn innocent children, many of them black, to regimes of terror. To call such a policy compassionate is a profound linguistic and moral distortion.

Not so long ago, it was commonplace for liberals to sanction such distortions. Thankfully, and with great effort (some of it expended on these pages), liberalism has largely rid itself of its propensity to equate moral decency with the indulgence of immoral behavior. Liberals, by and large, no longer assume that compassion means light sentences for criminals or allowing the able-bodied to claim government money absent a day's work. As Decatur shows, however, the battle is not completely won. Permissive liberalism, like all dying creeds, has its last bastion. How unfortunate that it is the American school.

> While [zero-tolerance] statutes have led to occasional excesses . . . in most cases the laws are working.

Reprinted from "The Fight's Not Over," *The New Republic*, December 6, 1999. Copyright © 1999 by The New Republic, Inc. Reprinted with permission from *The New Republic*.

Zero-Tolerance Laws Are Excessive

Nadine Strossen

For all the glossy teen dramas debuting on television this fall, the one program that most closely approximates reality for many high-school students today is HBO's gritty prison drama, *Oz.*

What with intrusive random searches—including strip searches and urinalysis drug testing—zero tolerance, snitch lines, seizures of private papers, drug-sniffing dogs, surveillance cameras, metal detectors, mandatory uniforms and on-site armed police officers, the schoolhouse these days is looking more and more like the jailhouse.

A Dangerous Loss of Rights

All of this follows, of course, in the wake of the shooting rampage at Columbine High School in Littleton, Colorado, in April 1999. It was tragic enough that, in this incident and several other school shootings between 1997 and 1999, 26 students were deprived of their lives. It compounds the tragedy, though, when these incidents are used to "justify" depriving millions of students of their rights.

In the post-Littleton backlash, the phones in American Civil Liberties Union (ACLU) offices all over the country have been ringing off the hook with calls from parents whose children have been suspended or expelled for such "dangerous" behavior as dyeing their hair blue, having body piercings or tattoos, wearing the Star of David on a necklace (supposedly it is some sort of "gang symbol"), or wearing a T-shirt bearing the name of that other notorious gang, the "Vegans." Worse yet, some students have been punished merely for daring to criticize their schools for punishing classmates who have worn such "threatening" items.

Defending these repressive policies, Chicago Public Schools Chief Paul Vallas commented, "We have an obligation to provide for [students'] safety first. When they're 18, then we can worry about some of these civil liberties issues."

As both a civil libertarian and an educator, I am troubled by that kind of statement. Of course, school safety should be a top priority. But safety and civil liberties are not mutually exclusive. And, just as adults are entitled to both safety and liberty, the same is true of our nation's youth.

> Safety and civil liberties are not mutually exclusive.

As the Supreme Court declared, in the landmark students' rights case that the ACLU won in 1969, *Tinker v. Des Moines School District:* "It can hardly be argued that . . . students shed their constitutional rights . . . at the schoolhouse gate."

Schoolhouse Hype

A number of educational organizations have echoed the ACLU's concern that the post-Columbine crackdown is an overreaction that is no better for students' safety or welfare than it is for their rights. Some examples include the National Association of School Administrators and the National Association of School Psychologists.

The media's sensationalized coverage of school violence has helped whip up exaggerated fears, which in turn spur officials to overreact, treating all students like potential perpetrators or victims of mass murder. Newsworthy as the Columbine and other school shootings are, they are not—fortunately—symptomatic of a nationwide trend. To the contrary, the many recent studies of school violence consistently document declines. Consider, for example, a recent report by the Justice Policy Institute, whose title tells it all: "School House Hype: School Shootings and the Real Risks Kids Face in America." This report shows that, between 1992 and 1995, there were an average of 42 violent deaths per year in schools; in contrast, in the last three years, that number dropped to 33.

> The media's sensationalized coverage of school violence has helped whip up exaggerated fears, which in turn spur officials to overreact.

This study further shows, sadly, that at least 2,000 children per year are killed by violence in their own homes, at the hands of their own parents or guardians. That is the equivalent of one Columbine every three days.

Far from addressing the real problems of violence for our nation's youth, though, public policy has been targeting schools, no doubt driven at least in part by media hype. According to one media watchdog, the Center for Media and Public Affairs, "[S]hootings at eight . . . public schools around the country generated . . . more than 10 hours of airtime within the first seven days of each incident, in addition to uncounted hours of live coverage and extensive followup discussions on the 24-hour cable news channels."

In addition to generating unfounded fears that "it could happen anywhere," the distorted media coverage tends to propel panic about all teenagers as potential terrorists—or at least all of those who wear black or favor Goth-themed Web sites, or who are otherwise "different."

A Nation at Risk II
In this vein, more schools are moving toward "profiling" their students, in yet another chilling parallel to a tactic

that comes from the criminal-justice field—and has been condemned as discriminatory and ineffective even in that context.

School officials are encouraged to single out for suspicion any student "who reflects the dark side of life" in written assignments, who "consistently prefers TV shows, movies or musical expressions of violent themes or acts," or who is involved with an "antisocial group on the fringe of peer acceptance," to name just a few problematic criteria—problematic because they may well lead to stereotyping, stigmatizing and even punishing students, just because they exercise First Amendment freedoms.

As I and other ACLU spokespeople regularly have been reminding school officials, "Different does not mean dangerous."

While I have warned against using profiles to identify students who endanger school safety, it is past time for parents and students to turn the tables and use their own profiles—based on criteria in the Constitution and Bill of Rights—to identify the schools that endanger students' rights. In addition to the danger signs that I have already mentioned, here are some other warning signals of schools that are hazardous for human rights (all of these are drawn from actual cases):

> The distorted media coverage [of school violence] tends to propel panic about all teenagers as potential terrorists.

- random searches of students' lockers, or removal of these lockers altogether.
- requiring that students' backpacks be transparent.
- censorship of school newspapers and/or yearbooks.
- punishment for Web sites created on students' home computers on their own time.

- attempts to regulate other off-campus behavior.
- school-sponsored religious exercises.
- summary suspension or expulsion without notice of charges or the right to respond.

Perhaps when school officials find themselves on the other end of the scrutiny, schools will start to look less like *Oz* and more like *My So-Called Life,* a mid-90s TV series that realistically depicted teenagers as full-fledged individuals, entitled to human dignity and civil liberties.

Reprinted from "My So-Called Rights," by Nadine Strossen, Intellectual-Capital.com, September 30, 1999. Reprinted with permission. Article available at www.intellectualcapital.com/issues/issue306/item6640.asp.

Chapter 2

Teens and Guns

How Guns Exacerbate Teen Violence

Griffin Dix

Guns are the leading cause of death among American males age fifteen to twenty-four, explains Griffin Dix. According to Dix, the presence of guns in the home greatly increases the chances of homicides and suicides, as well as accidental deaths. Citing a 1995 study, Dix points out that as many as one in twelve high school students reported carrying a gun to school and students rank the fear of gun violence as their greatest concern. Dix is a member of the Executive Committee of the Silent March Against Gun Violence. His fifteen-year-old son was killed in an unintentional shooting while visiting a friend's house.

When my beloved 15-year-old son was killed by a handgun, I had no idea gunshots are the leading cause of death of American males age 15 to 24. One of his best friends decided to show him the gun his father kept loaded next to his bed. The boy took out the clip that had bullets in it and put in an empty clip. He did not know there was still a bullet hidden in the chamber. He pulled the trigger and was shocked to see that he had fired a bullet into my son's shoulder and into his heart. His

Reprinted from "Some Facts, Some Opinions About Youth and Guns," by Griffin Dix. Reprinted with permission from www.cyberteens.com; article available at www.cyberteens.com/ezine/issue14/fresh/dix.html.

death was a senseless but predictable accident caused by poor gun design, improper storage of a gun by the gun owner, and irresponsible gun marketing.

The father believed the handgun would somehow protect his family. He had trained his son in its use. He did not know a gun in the home increases the probability of a gun homicide there by 2.7 times, and the probability of a gun suicide by almost five times.

Handguns as Protection?

More than 40 percent of American homes have guns. In too many homes the youth know how to get the gun. And the gun that they get is not likely to be a safe product. Not only is the gun too often accessible; frequently it does not have a trigger lock, or an effective chamber loaded indicator that a child can understand. Guns should have locks built-in so only the owner can fire them.

Why are guns so unsafe? Because our own U.S. legislature specifically exempted guns from regulation by the Consumer Products Safety Commission when it was formed in 1972. Because guns are not made safe, there are a shocking 1200 to 1500 accidental gun deaths per year in the U.S. Products that kill far fewer people have been regulated for safety.

> Most Americans . . . want stricter regulation of guns.

Most Americans, over 70 percent, want stricter regulation of guns and do not approve of their legislators listening to pro-gun special interest groups and disregarding public safety. For example, a poll in California found that 85 percent of voters favored regulating guns like other consumer products. Fortunately many voters are beginning to understand the public health side of the issue and turning pro-gun legislators out of office.

Gun Suicide

The victim may be the shooter himself when he gets depressed and turns the gun on himself. As you see from the national numbers of gun deaths, gun suicide is even more common than gun homicide. Gun suicide is a family tragedy frequently hidden from sight. Mental turmoil is often a part of the teen years. If a teenager has a gun at hand and becomes depressed (as we all do at some time), and if he acts impulsively, he may destroy all possibility of recovery by a "permanent 'solution' to a temporary problem." If the suicide were attempted by some other means there is a much greater chance of the life being saved so the problem could be dealt with.

> Homes without guns are safer than homes that have guns.

How to Protect Yourself from Guns in Homes

Make sure your home is safe. Homes without guns are safer than homes that have guns. If there is a gun of any kind in your home, make sure it is stored locked with the ammunition locked away in a different place.

If you see a gun, don't touch it. If a friend touches it, tell him to put it down. Tell a responsible adult in that home and tell your parents. Certainly, under responsible supervision, target shooting can be safe. But never lose sight of how quickly and easily a gun can destroy lives.

Teens and Adults Need to Talk About the Reality of Guns

On TV or at the movies, we see heroes using guns frequently. The hero blasts away with his arsenal; he wins. If he is injured it is only a minor matter. The death, the horror, the grieving, the destruction of families is not shown. Guns seem to be instant access to power and respect. But kids need to recognize the dangers of guns and how different things can be from the movies.

If we understand the specific nature of the public health risk to children in the U.S., we can work toward public education and legislation that will save many of these young lives. The

easy availability of handguns causes many accidents and suicides, both of which are clearly public health issues. But it is important to recognize that even the gun homicides are often more
a public health issue than specifically a crime issue. Most people
who kill with a gun are not "criminals" with a felony record, and
most are not committing a premeditated crime such as a robbery.
Frequently the shooter is a person who gets uncontrollably angry and, if a gun is at hand, what would have been an argument
becomes a gun homicide. The victims tend to be the shooter's
own relatives and friends.

Don Wright. © 1981 Tribune Information Services. All rights reserved.
Reprinted with permission.

Kids are fascinated by guns but they are also worried by guns
and violence. A 1995 survey showed that kids age seven to 17 say
that violence and guns are the greatest threat to their lives. Because guns are such a part of kids lives and worries, parents and
kids should talk about these problems. Many schools now ask
kids to pledge not to resort to violence. The cycle of violence and
retaliation leads to tragic results for everyone involved. Talk
about how to solve arguments without violence of any kind.

For Junior and Senior High School students there is another new issue seldom faced by their parent's generation. A 1995 national survey showed eight percent of students (one in 12) reported carrying a firearm for fighting or self-defense at least once in the previous 30 days. If a friend carries a gun, it puts them and everyone around them at risk. Too many things can go wrong. About 80 percent of people killed with a gun knew the person who pulled the trigger. For your safety, separate yourself from a person with a gun. For their safety and that of others, tell them to get rid of the gun. If they think they need a gun for protection, tell them there are other ways of protection that work better, such as avoiding walking alone, taking a self defense class, carrying a personal alarm, etc. Avoid people and places where violence is likely to break out. Have the strength to walk away from a conflict.

> The easy availability of handguns causes many accidents and suicides.

Reducing Gun Violence

It's outrageous that our legislators refuse to regulate guns the way we regulate other consumer products. Guns should not be exempt from regulation by the Consumer Products Safety Commission. Another mistake our legislators made is to allow domestic manufacture of cheap, poor quality Saturday Night Specials, when they outlawed importation of these "junk guns" that are most likely to get into the hands of an angry youth or a low life criminal. We could save many lives simply by closing this loophole and forbidding U.S. companies from making these "junk guns."

Youth are affected by guns and they can let their legislators know what should be done to make our lives safer.

The historical success of some U.S. gun regulations and the experience of other countries prove well-planned regulations can save lives. A national one-gun-a-month law would help prevent gun-running where people buy many guns in states with lax laws then sell them illegally in states with stricter laws.

We need better laws to protect all Americans, not only kids. We regulate cars because they are extremely dangerous. Similarly, we need to register handguns, license gun owners, and make them take responsibility for the damage their handguns do, including having liability insurance. We need laws that force handgun manufacturers to make them safer.

Youth and Firearms

- In 1994, firearm injuries were the second leading cause of death for young people, 10 to 24 years of age and the third leading cause of death for persons aged 2 to 34.
- Nearly 29% of those who died from firearm injuries in 1994 were 15- to 24-years-old.
- In 1995, 7.6% or 1 in 12 students in a national survey reported carrying a firearm for fighting or self-defense at least once in the previous 30 days. In 1990, this was true of 4.1% or 1 in 24 students.
- Between 1985 and 1994, the risk of dying from a firearm injury has more than doubled for teenagers 15 to 19 years of age.

Centers for Disease Control, available at www.cdc.gov/ncipc/factsheets/fafacts.htm.

All guns should be "childproof" with locks built in. That would also help reduce the problem of stolen guns. One-third of guns used in crime are stolen guns. (Notice that none of these suggestions involve taking guns away or preventing adults from buying a gun. But hopefully that decision will be made considering all the dangers.)

Reducing gun violence will save tax money. Tax dollars pay over 80 percent of the cost of treating gunshot wounds. Recent research indicates the total cost of U.S. gun violence, including lost productivity due to premature death, is about $20.4 billion each year.

It is not just tragic, but also shameful that guns are the second leading cause of death for young people 10 to 24. The high U.S. rate of childhood death by guns is preventable, unlike death, for example, by a disease for which there is no cure. The epidemic of youth gun deaths is a social and political problem that can be reduced by talking about guns and violence, and by getting involved to enact reasonable regulations that will save American children from the danger of gun violence in all its forms. People who care about kids and about public safety need to act now.

The Easy Availability of Guns in the Inner City

Shanikqua Crawford

Every day an average of fourteen children age nineteen and under are killed by guns, writes Shanikqua Crawford. Part of the reason for the high rate of gun fatalities among teens, Crawford explains, is that guns are easily available to most teens. Also, Crawford notes, many teens, especially those in tough neighborhoods, mistakenly believe that carrying a gun will protect them from violence. Crawford is a writer for *New Youth Connections,* a magazine written by and for teenagers.

L ately, when you pick up the newspaper or watch the news, you see teenagers and even younger kids who are shooting each other or shooting up their schools. Since last October, at least 15 people have died in a string of school shootings around the country.

Is this a trend? Is there something wrong with these kids? Or is it too easy for a teenager to get a gun?

Buying a Gun Is Easy

If you talk to teens around the city many will tell you that buying a gun is simple.

"Buying a gun is as easy for a teenager as it is for them to buy smokes," said Ebony King, 15, of the Bronx. And that's where I think we start looking at the problem.

The latest episode of teen gun violence to hit the news happened in June 1998, when a 14-year-old boy shot and wounded two adults at Armstrong High School in Richmond, Virginia, as the adults were trying to break up a fight. The adults, a history teacher and a volunteer helper, were not the intended victims.

> Buying a gun is as easy for a teenager as it is for them to buy smokes.

A month earlier in Springfield, Oregon, a boy who had been suspended for bringing a gun to school returned the next day and opened fire with a semiautomatic rifle in the school cafeteria.

The boy, 15-year-old Kipland Kinkel, killed two students and wounded 22 others. In addition, his parents were found shot to death, allegedly by the young boy.

And in March 1998, 11-year-old Andrew Golden and 13-year-old Mitchell Johnson hid in the nearby woods outside of Westside Middle School near Jonesboro, Arkansas, with 10 guns and fired 22 shots at unsuspecting classmates and teachers.

Four girls and a teacher were killed and 10 people were wounded. Their reason—a young girl broke up with one of the boys and he wanted revenge.

Guns Kill Kids Every Single Day

There are three things that each of these crimes has in common:
1. They were committed by kids.
2. Everyone who took part in these crimes was able to get and use a gun.
3. They were committed at schools.

According to the Coalition to Stop Gun Violence, every single day an average of 14 children age 19 and under are killed with a gun. Firearm injuries are the second leading cause of death among youth ages 10–24 nationwide.

And the number of young people dying by gunfire is on the rise. According to the Department of Justice, the number of youth killed with a firearm increased by 153% between 1985 and 1995 (the number of juvenile homicide victims killed with something other than a gun increased by 9%).

As we have been witnessing around the country, guns are playing a big role in young people dying.

Nowadays, it seems like what's important to teens is being able to have and use a gun. It's like an American Express card— you can't leave home without it.

Guns Give Punks Courage

In my neighborhood, in the Bronx, it seems that mostly all the guys between ages 14 and 21 carry guns. Some do it because they're drug dealers, and others, I'd say, because they're punks.

With their guns they feel high and mighty, but take them away and they're left with nothing. All they think about is how hip and bad they are with their weapons, but what they fail to realize is how fearful and afraid they'd be without them.

Another reason they have a gun is because it's very easy to obtain them. I know because every teen I interviewed said so.

These teens are not the only young people who feel this way.

According to a recent national poll of students in grades 6 to 12 by the Office of Juvenile Justice and Delinquency Prevention, 59% replied that they "could get a gun if they wanted," while 35% said it would take them less than an hour to get a gun.

> Every single day an average of 14 children age 19 and under are killed with a gun.

Betty, 16, of Harlem, said, "It is real easy. You can get an older friend to get it for you. You can just get it on the low. You gotta have connections. It's like if you walk into a liquor store and they're not supposed to sell you liquor, but there's always somebody who'll sell it to you for money."

In a playful but serious tone, Marcus Bryan, 15, of the Bronx, also explained how simple it is for a teenager to purchase a gun.

"My friend is going to purchase me a piece right now," he said laughing. "Nah, I'm just playing, but seriously, that's how easy it is. You can get a gun anywhere, yo. They sell them in some check cashing places."

The Prevalence of Weapons-Related Violence

The following statistics about teens and weapons are taken from a 1995 survey conducted by Roper Starch Worldwide.

- Seventeen percent of students in small cities currently carry a weapon, compared to 12 percent in the suburbs and rural areas and 9 percent in large cities.
- Seventeen percent of students claim to have been robbed at gun- or knifepoint.
- Fifty-one percent know someone who carries a weapon to school or in their neighborhood.
- Forty-one percent know someone in their own home who has a gun.
- Thirty-four percent know someone who has been shot.

I was surprised by the places where teens can get guns. Teens also told me they could get guns from their parents, older friends, drug dealers and crackheads. All you have to do is know where to go and who to go to.

Teens Think They Need Protection

Teens mostly carry guns for protection. They think no one will mess with them if they are "protected," and they think they have to be protected nowadays just to walk down the street. As Nini, 15, from Brooklyn puts it, "Protection against every-body–gangs, everybody, your peers. You can never trust any-body, so you have to be protected."

They believe there are many people out there who pose a problem for them, and a gun would be the easiest way to solve their problems.

Sometimes teens even carry guns to help out a friend. One such incident occurred with Nini. This guy she knew brought a gun to their school. He was called to the office, so he gave her the gun to hold so he wouldn't get caught with it.

When she got called to the office, she passed it on to the next person. Nini described it as a cycle.

"Whoever was called to the office would pass it on, " she said.

Ain't Nothing Good on the Streets

Teens also carry guns because they're members of gangs. When Betty asked if she carried a gun, she replied, "Not now, but before, yeah, because I was involved with gangs and I was living on the street and ain't nothing good on the streets."

"Another reason [teens carry guns] is to be down," Ebony said. "They feel that if they carry a gun, everybody will respect them and they gonna have props."

This interested me because it shows teens carry guns just to be part of a clique or even to get respect from others.

The Death of a Friend

Some kids I spoke with think that gun violence among everyone, but especially teens, is wrong.

They believe that there is no need for it because it only causes pain and suffering for everyone—not only for the victim but for the victim's family, friends, and maybe even strangers who hear about it.

Marteen Baker, 15, of the Bronx, has experienced the death of a friend due to teen gun violence. Her next door neighbor, who was 18, was shot and killed by another 18 year old over a misunderstanding about a bike.

"He didn't deserve to die over a bike," she said. "People

should use fists to fight and not guns."

Another teenager I interviewed said her older brother's best friend, who was 15 or 16, was shot and killed for an unknown reason, but she thinks it had something to do with drugs.

"It was very depressing," she said. "I wouldn't kill nobody because I know how it feels to have somebody taken away from you, and I wouldn't want nobody to feel that pain."

Nini has also lost a close friend to gunfire. Her best friend's brother, who was 14 years old, was shot by three teenagers and two adults over an infamous drug spot. The teens who took part in the killing were 13, 15, and 17.

> Teenagers should be able to live normal lives and not have to feel the pain of a boyfriend or friend getting shot for no good reason.

Nini said the death of her friend make her more aware and cautious about who she can trust.

Guns Are Made for Killing

Although he has never personally experienced the loss of a loved one or friend because of gun violence, Marcus feels strongly about the subject.

"[There's] no need for guns because guns are made for killing," he said.

Looking at all the gun violence, we can come to the conclusion that what Marcus says is true. In all of the above cases, children were killed by other children, and there really was no need for it. Children are murdered every day and over petty things—a drug spot, a bike, getting dumped.

Our neighborhoods should be places we can go outside and live normally without seeing bitter surroundings.

Teenagers should be able to live normal lives and not have to feel the pain of a boyfriend or friend getting shot for no good reason.

But instead of dwelling on the fact that these teens are shooting other teens, we should try to understand more clearly *why* they are killing other teens, *where* they get their weapons, and *what* we can do to help them and their victims.

This way, a solution can be found to try to stop this problem, and these distressed teens can shoot some knowledge into their brains instead of shooting each other's brains out.

Weapons Can't Protect You

Latonya Williams

In the following selection, Latonya Williams recalls the shooting death of a friend and how his death—the result of a senseless argument—changed her outlook on violence. Before her friend met his violent end, Williams never thought much about teens who carry guns and knives. In fact, she carried a blade herself. Like most teens who carry guns and knives, Williams carried her box cutter for protection. After her friend was killed, however, Williams realized that carrying a weapon offers no protection. She believes teens who are preoccupied with weapons would be better off devoting their time and energy toward education. Williams is a writer for *Foster Care Youth United,* a magazine that covers topics pertinent to youths in foster care.

Journal Entry: February 28, 1996

My good friend Dwayne was killed early Sunday morning February 25, 1996, at a party around his block in Brooklyn. It seems that this boy bumped Dwayne, they started arguing, and then they started fighting. The guy pulled out a gun and shot Dwayne point blank in the chest, in cold blood. The last time I saw him was nine days before, on my birthday.

I'm very upset over this. I don't understand why my friend had to lose his life over something so petty. I also don't understand how God could let this happen. I want all this violence to stop before some other teenage boy or girl loses his/her life to violence.

I don't know if writing about it is going to help, but I'm willing to try anything. Maybe some other teenager will read my story and decide to talk matters out instead of blowing his opponent away.

Right now I'm so mad at the guy who killed Dwayne I could shoot him point blank, just like he shot Dwayne. I feel this boy doesn't deserve to live. He had no right to take Dwayne's life like that. He hurt a lot of people by his act of violence.

Dwayne was going to be 17 soon and he should have lived to see his birthday. Why couldn't God work this miracle and allow Dwayne to live, instead of dying in an ambulance from a bullet piercing his heart?

I wish Dwayne was still alive. I hope there is a heaven so I will have something to look forward to, besides being up there with my mother and grandparents.

I wish there was something I could have done to prevent it. If I could go back in time, I would have prevented him from dying. I don't care if I had to take the bullet. Dwayne would be alive and well if I could have helped it. I know it sounds delirious, but I am hurt, mad, and disappointed in the world today. Most of all, I want my friend back.

R.I.P Dwayne
June 20, 1979–
February 25, 1996

Love Always,
Latonya

On February 28, 1996, in the journal entry above, I wrote about how upset I was with the guy who killed Dwayne. I was so upset I wanted to kill him. I've come to realize that my attitude was self-destructive. The only thing that attitude would have gotten me was a cell in prison or six feet under. I still miss Dwayne a lot, but I know now that as I hold on to my memories of him, he will never die.

Obviously, Dwayne's killer was very ignorant to think he could kill someone just because he was disrespected. He confessed to the cops two days before the wake. I don't know what happened to him after that, but now I feel sorry for him.

By making Dwayne a statistic, he also became a statistic in the growing problem of Black-on-Black crime. He is just another Black youth who bites the dust.

Education Is the Key

There are too many ignorant teenagers who don't understand that there is more to life than the hardships around their block or standing on the corner smoking weed. I believe education is the key to stopping violence. Life does get better once you get an education.

I can understand how life gets discouraging when you try to do the right thing (legal thing) and all you seem to get is bad luck. But kids should stay in school and try to get the best education, so they can leave the hardships in the neighborhood and go off to college. With a college degree you

> Pumping a bullet into a guy's chest because he looked at you hard is stupid.

can get money! and not worry about being bagged by the cops.

I also believe there should be smaller schools and classes where kids can have one-on-one relationship with their teachers. A lot of teachers in bigger high schools cannot tend to the students who need extra help. When kids don't get the help they need, they feel discouraged and give up.

A Weapon Won't Protect

Teenagers in schools where the teachers really care about them will understand that pumping a bullet into a guy's chest because he looked at you hard is stupid. They'll understand the consequences of their actions and look toward the future. Kids without an education do not feel they have a future, so they act on their immediate emotions. Kids have to believe they're going to make it to 18 and beyond.

My whole outlook on violence has changed since Dwayne's death. I care a lot more about it than I used to. I now understand that a blade or a gun cannot protect me from getting killed.

Firearms and Black Youth

Black youths have higher rates of firearm homicide than any other racial/ethnic group.

The firearms homicide rate for black youths is more than twice the rate for Hispanic youths, more than three times the rate for Asian youths and nearly 10 times the rate for white youths.

- In 1997, black males, 17 years of age and younger, had a firearms homicide rate of 10.3 per 100,000.
- In 1997, black males, aged 10 to 17 years, had a firearms homicide rate of 22.3 per 100,000.

Firearms homicide is the second leading cause of death for black males 17 years of age and younger.

Violence Policy Center, available at www.vpc.org/press/0004fact.htm.

Before I never really had an opinion on violence and weapon carrying. If someone carried a blade or a gun I didn't care, because it didn't affect me. Now I realize it does. If someone carries a gun and decides to shoot their enemy, that bullet might miss them and hit me or my loved one.

A lot of people feel that by carrying a weapon they're protected. They need a wake-up call, because if somebody really wanted to kill or hurt you, they would do it. A weapon can't protect you.

Let's say Dwayne had a gun on him and shot the guy first. Dwayne would have spent the rest of his life in jail. That gun would have taken away his life in a different way, just like it took away his killer's life.

Carrying a weapon might even cause beef. Some guys and girls don't know how to act when they're strapped. They brag and boast about the weapon they have. They're quick to threaten their enemies.

I know first-hand that when someone is threatened, they begin to carry a weapon or take action.

A Close Call

About two years ago, I carried a boxcutter for protection. When I was in ninth grade, me and my friend had a beef with these girls in our school. I went to the store and bought a boxcutter just in case those girls tried to "herb" me when I was by myself.

I never had to use it, although I came close one day. One of my friends had a fight with this girl by my school and I thought her friend was about to jump in. I took off my coat, pulled out my blade, and was about to attack. People pulled us back and I didn't have to use it, which was a good thing. If I had sliced my enemy, she probably would have tried to kill me and a lot of people would have gotten hurt.

My old enemies and I are peoples now and everything is squashed. As time passed we stopped arguing with each other and started worrying about more important things. If there are confrontations, people should leave weapons out of it. It's safer that way and everyone ends up with their lives.

> A weapon can't protect you.

Last summer I lost my blade and I never bought a new one. I feel no need for it anymore, and I was immature back then. Two years ago I didn't really need that blade. If I wanna fight now, I'm just gonna fight fair and get on with my life.

Still Missing Him

If no one carried weapons, there wouldn't be anyone to protect yourself from. Everyone would be forced to shoot the fifth and whoever wins, wins. At least you'd have your life.

I still miss Dwayne, but the days are better now. It gets hard for me when I think about him dying so violently, but I realize he's in heaven chillin'. I'm gonna end this story just like I ended my journal entry.

R.I.P Dwayne
June 20, 1979–
February 25, 1996

Love Always,
Latonya

Why I Carry a Gun

Anonymous

In the following essay, an anonymous seventeen-year-old from Brooklyn, New York, explains why he carries a gun. The author lives in Flatbush, a tough neighborhood in Brooklyn that is plagued with violence, and feels that he needs a gun for protection. Though the author has owned numerous guns, he also points out that having a gun can bring trouble as well. Sometimes when a teen has a gun, he or she is tempted to do something stupid, like show off or take revenge. Having a gun also increases your chances of getting shot because someone may decide to shoot you before you get the chance to shoot them.

I got my first gun when I was 13 because I thought it was cool. I didn't really have any use for one at the time but I know a lot of people who had guns and I wanted one too. The gun was a .25 automatic. I got it from my friend for $100.

It's easy to get a gun in my neighborhood. There are guys all over who sell them. I never used mine to hurt anybody. The most I did was go up on the roof of an abandoned building and shoot a few cans and bottles.

I'm 17 now and my reasons for carrying a gun have changed. I live in a really rough area of Brooklyn and I've seen a lot of things. Once I want to a party in Flatbush. Everybody was dancing and having a food time and then shots rang out and everyone ran outside. (Luckily no one got hurt.) Another time I heard shots outside my window. I looked out and saw this man chasing another man down the street, shooting. I've been stuck up a couple of times myself and friends of mine have been shot dead.

Once I shot a guy in self-defense. I was at a party minding my business when a boy walked up to me and said he heard

Children and Teen Firearm Deaths over Time

	Total	Homicide	Suicide	Accident	Unknown Intent
1979	3,710	1,651	1,220	726	113
1980	3,749	1,743	1,214	689	103
1981	3,589	1,660	1,213	604	112
1982	3,332	1,498	1,207	550	77
1983	2,962	1,238	1,150	504	70
1984	3,030	1,289	1,114	552	75
1985	3,169	1,322	1,256	519	72
1986	3,349	1,513	1,293	472	71
1987	3,400	1,573	1,281	467	79
1988	3,974	1,953	1,387	543	91
1989	4,384	2,367	1,380	567	70
1990	4,935	2,852	1,476	541	66
1991	5,329	3,247	1,436	551	95
1992	5,353	3,336	1,426	501	90
1993	5,715	3,625	1,460	526	104
1994	5,793	3,579	1,565	512	137
1995	5,254	3,249	1,450	440	115
1996	4,613	2,836	1,309	376	92
1997	4,205	2,562	1,262	306	75
Total	**79,845**	**43,093**	**25,099**	**9,946**	**1,707**

Source: National Center for Health Statistics, Division of Vital Statistics.

that I was messing with his girl.

"What the hell you talking about?" I said. "I don't know you nor your damn girl."

He turned to some other guys and said, "Yo, I got him." I knew something was gonna go down, so I left.

After I got outside, I noticed some guys following me. I ran and hid in a bushy area until they had gone by. All the time my hand was on my gun—just in case.

After they were gone, I stepped out from where I was hiding, and just then another guy came around the corner heading in the same direction as his friends. He saw me and reached into his coat. I fired twice. He fell on the ground with his gun in his hand. If I hadn't shot him first I might not be here today.

I've had lots of guns. I just plain lost the first one. After that there were a couple of times when I had to get rid of a gun because I was scared the cops were going to find it on me. Cops in my neighborhood are always stopping a group of kids and searching them. One time I was hanging out with my friends and I saw the cops drive by. I had a feeling they were coming back so I dropped my gun down the sewer. They did come back and found guns on all my friends and drove then off to jail.

> It's easy to get a gun in my neighborhood.

Later that same night I want out to get something to eat and this group of kids robbed me. One of them stuck a gun in my stomach and they pushed me up against the wall and went digging through my pockets. They took all my money and ran off. I was so mad that I went home and got another gun I had and went back out after them. I didn't find them. I was glad I didn't because that would've brought trouble on me from the cops.

Guns Bring Trouble

There are a lot of ways just having a gun can bring trouble. For one thing, you have to be careful where you get it. You don't want a gun with "bodies on it." With a gun in your pocket you can also be tempted to do stupid things. Some people use their guns to show off and make themselves look big—that's foolishness. You might shoot someone you don't like or try to take revenge. And if other people know you have a gun they're more likely to try to shoot you before you get the chance to shoot them.

Point of Contention: Should Teenagers Have Access to Guns?

In the wake of the high profile mass shootings that occurred in American schools between 1996 and 1999, the debate surrounding the causes of teen violence has frequently focused on the availability of guns. Some critics, such as freelance writer William Goodwin, point out that the easy availability of firearms exacerbates teen violence by turning ordinary fights between teens into gun battles. Others, like Robert W. Lee, a contributing editor to *New American* magazine, contend that the negative incidents involving teens and firearms are exaggerated. Gun advocates contend that there are many more positive examples of responsible firearms use by teens than the anti-gun lobby will admit.

Teens Should Not Carry Guns

William Goodwin

One major contributor to the escalation of teen violence that experts do generally agree upon is the easy availability of guns. According to a 1996 report by the American Academy of Child and Adolescent Psychiatry, every day in the United States ten children under the age of nineteen are killed with handguns in homicides, suicides, or accidents. Many more are injured by guns. In fact, according to the Center of Prevent Handgun Violence, fourteen out of fifteen juvenile murders were shootings in 1992.

Guns figure in more than 75 percent of adolescent homicides and more than half of teenage suicides. An astounding number of children either own a gun or know how to get one. A national survey by the Centers for Disease Control and Prevention in Atlanta found that 4 percent of the country's high school students had carried a gun at least once in the month prior to the survey. In some schools the figure was considerably higher. Up to one-third of the students who said they had taken a gun to school reported that they had actually fired their guns at another person at least once.

By all indications, guns are easier than ever to obtain. In Chicago, San Diego, and New York, just to name three examples of cities with laws designed to make it difficult to acquire a gun quickly, police on gang details say that a kid can get a cheap pistol within two hours for as little as twenty dollars. And every city has teens who are well versed in gun availability. In a 1996 article in the *San Diego Union-Tribune,* a member of the San Diego Police Department's gang unit described a tenth grader who could name every popular gun model ranging from easily concealed Raven semiautomatic to an Intratec mini–machine gun. The teen added, "As long as you got the money, you can get a gun."

> Every day in the United States ten children under the age of nineteen are killed with handguns in homicides, suicides, or accidents.

Gun Violence Soars

With so many guns currently in the hands of young people, routine fights often turn into gun battles. Fearing for their safety, more and more teens are taking up arms in a brutal cycle of escalating violence. In 1992, according to the Centers for Disease Control and Prevention, the nationwide number of juvenile murders not involving guns grew 20 percent while the number that did involve guns grew 300 percent.

Quoted in a 1996 U.S. Department of Justice Fact Sheet, a probation officer in Los Angeles, who supervises many juvenile gang members, estimated that 80 percent had been wounded by gunfire at least once in their lives and over 20 percent have been shot more than once. "The type of firepower and the access to guns have both increased radically even as the age of the shooters has dropped," stated the probation officer.

A Political Response to Teen Gun Violence

A growing number of the nation's political leaders, convinced that the easy availability of handguns is the driving force behind the growth in teen violence, are looking for ways to reverse this dangerous trend. On October 10, 1996, eighty-four senators from both political parties joined President Bill Clinton in not only urging all young Americans to voluntarily sign a pledge designed to decrease gun violence, but also they asked the youth of America to make the following vow:

> I pledge I will never bring a gun to school; that I will never use a gun to settle a dispute; and that I will use my influence with my friends to keep them from using guns to settle disputes.

The principal author of this pledge, Senator Bill Bradley, summed up the feeling among many Americans when he said in a speech to Congress:

> An epidemic of violence is ensnaring our children at an alarming rate. It is time to make it unfashionable to resolve a dispute with a gun. It is time to give young people in this country a chance to stand up and retake their schools and their neighborhoods.

Teens Can Use Guns in a Responsible Manner

Robert W. Lee

Advocates of gun control are inclined to portray firearms in the worst possible light while ignoring the positive aspects of gun ownership and use. They will, for example, focus on the million or so violent gun incidents committed by offenders annually, while disregarding the estimated 2.5 million-plus successful defensive uses of firearms each year. Such self-serving bias is equivalent to condemning prescription drugs because tens of thousands of persons die each year from adverse drug reactions, while ignoring the more numerous instances in which such drugs save lives.

The tendency to ignore evidence that challenges planks of the anti-gun agenda has surfaced in the wake of recent shooting incidents at schools in Arkansas, Kentucky, and Mississippi. The major media and gun control zealots have sought, for example, to create the impression that when minors use guns other than for supervised hunting or target shooting, the results are inevitably disastrous. That misleading assumption was also evident in a 1994 public service advertisement (PSA) about children and guns run on several television stations in Utah. It featured the president of the Utah Chiefs of Police Association asking rhetorically, "When do you think a child, or teenager, should have a gun?" and sternly warning that "the only reason for a child to have a gun is a dangerous one."

Safety Measure

But a few days before the PSA appeared, the *Salt Lake Tribune* reported an incident in Tulsa, Oklahoma in which 13-year-old Jarrod Barnes, who had been properly trained in the use of firearms, probably saved his own life and those of three younger brothers who sought refuge in a bedroom after an intruder burst into their home while their parents were away. According to the *Tribune,* while a brother dialed 911 the interloper tried to force the bedroom door open, at which point Jarrod "went for his stepfather's .357 Magnum and fired through the bedroom door, striking the man in the chest." The man "stumbled into the front yard and collapsed dead." A pocket knife and 15-inch screwdriver were found on the body.

The two oldest brothers had attended gun safety classes sponsored by the Oklahoma Wildlife Conservation Department. The boys' stepfather told reporters that he considered "the older boys to be experts with firearms," adding: "We taught him [Jarrod] where to aim at the door if the door rattled. He did exactly as he was instructed." He speculated that "the firearms training the boys received probably saved their lives." No charges were filed against the parents for allowing Jarrod and his brothers to have access to the gun that may have saved their lives. . . .

> Gun control zealots have sought . . . to create the impression that when minors use guns other than for supervised hunting or target shooting, the results are inevitably disastrous.

Exercising the Right

There have been many instances of minors employing handguns or rifles to defend themselves or loved ones from injury or death from other persons or wild animals. Here are a handful of examples, gleaned from news accounts and the monthly "The Armed Citizen" column of the National Rifle Association's *American Rifleman* magazine:

• In 1996, although her parents and a deputy sheriff were at the scene, a 15-year-old Cookeville, Tennessee, teen was forced to defend herself when an abusive ex-boyfriend eluded the deputy, kicked in the door of the home in which she was hiding, and came after her while she was calling 911. She had the phone in one hand, but a Ruger .44 magnum in the other. A single fatal shot saved her from certain harm and possible death.

• In 1992, 14-year-old Clint Reynolds of Central, Alaska, was awakened by noise from a scuffle between an uncle and a grizzly bear attempting to climb through the window of the family home. Young Reynolds quickly loaded his .357 magnum revolver and fired seven shots into the bear, mortally wounding the marauding animal.

• In 1992, two teenage girls were asleep at home in Bakersfield, California, when two armed men kicked in the door and demanded money. As one of the men grabbed a wallet, one of the girls grabbed a handgun and opened fire, mortally wounding the other thug. His accomplice fled.

• In 1994, a father and son teamed up to thwart a burglary. Walter Bracken and son Daniel of Albuquerque, New Mexico, noticed a strange truck near another family member's home. When they went to investigate, two intruders attempted to run over the father, but Daniel, armed with a .30-30 rifle, fired several shots, wounding the driver. The other man fled. Police investigators concluded that Daniel had acted properly in self-defense.

• In 1993, after the family home had been burgled several times, 17-year-old Darren Yakunovich of Kipton, Ohio, stayed home from school in the hope of apprehending the burglar. The thief did indeed strike again (it was an erstwhile friend), but when he entered an upstairs room Daniel ended his crime career, at least temporarily, by holding him at gunpoint until the police arrived.

Youthful Soldiers

In our nation's early years, young people often served courageously and competently in the military. One particularly important battle of the Civil War is worth noting. The Virginia Military Institute, founded in 1839, is the nation's oldest state-supported military college. Its graduates have fought in every American conflict since the Mexican War, and the service of its entire cadet corps during the 1864 Civil War battle of New Market, Virginia, marks the only occasion in U.S. history in which an entire student body has fought as a unit in pitched battle. The 257 cadets included many minors, the youngest of whom was 15.

> Not all young people who wield firearms for purposes other than hunting or target shooting do so in an irresponsible manner.

An account of the battle by Colonel William Couper, VMI's official historiographer, in *The VMI New Market Cadets* (1933) describes how on May 15, 1864 the "deadly fire of shells, grape, canister and bullets, to which the corps was subjected . . . did not cause it to retreat or even fall back temporarily." Instead, it "began, for the first time, to fire upon the enemy." At one point, when a command was given to the corps to charge, it "was obeyed, not only with alacrity, but with enthusiasm." Indeed, "So eager were the cadets to charge the enemy, 100 or 150 yards off, that it was difficult for them to find time to load and shoot their old-fashioned muzzle loading muskets."

The retreating Northerners were pursued until the VMI corps "was halted by the order of [Confederate Major] General [John C.] Breckinridge." This important Southern victory, Couper notes, "temporarily preserved the Shenandoah's resources for the Confederacy." Ten of the VMI cadets either died during the battle or later from wounds they received. Another 47 suffered non-fatal wounds. The Institute eventually purchased much of the battlefield, on which it erected the nation's largest Civil War memorial to honor the youthful New Market heroes.

The incidents cited above are not intended to minimize the problem of youth violence, including gun-related violence. They are simply a reminder that not all young people who wield firearms for purposes other than hunting or target shooting do so in an irresponsible manner.

Excerpted from "Good Kids with Guns," by Robert W. Lee, *The New American,* May 25, 1998. Reprinted with permission from *The New American.*

Chapter 3

Violence in Relationships

Teen

Decisions

Why Teens Get Involved in Abusive Relationships

Erin Shaw

Teens' inexperience with dating, coupled with their unfamiliarity as to what constitutes a healthy relationship, leads some of them to believe that violence in a relationship is normal, writes *Arizona Republic* reporter Erin Shaw. In addition, teens are under an enormous amount of pressure to "fit in" with their friends, and many teens will stay with abusive partners because they fear losing popularity in their peer group.

At 17, Rochelle dreams about pizza parties.

She yearns for the normal, fun things teenagers love—talking with friends, laughing about boys, planning expeditions to the mall.

But normality has seemed out of reach for Rochelle, who already has been physically and mentally abused by several boyfriends. At 16, it drove her to heroin and a suicide attempt.

"My boyfriend used to pick me up and pin me to the brick wall at school, holding me by my neck," Rochelle said.

She flinched as she remembered how other students walked by, either ignoring her or laughing as she tried to escape.

Rochelle's case is more severe than most. But experts say dat-

Reprinted from "Dating Violence Makes Nightmare of Teen Years," by Erin Shaw, *The Arizona Republic*, July 5, 1998. Reprinted with permission.

ing violence is a reality for one of every three high school students.

Dating abuse can be verbal, emotional, physical or sexual, social workers and school counselors say. It can begin with name-calling or a simple push. It can end with beatings, rape, even the threat of death.

"I think it's an issue and it's not always reported," says Susan Jenkin, counselor at Canyon Del Oro High School in Tucson, Arizona. She says teens are afraid to ask for help because they believe the abuse they're suffering is "normal."

Teens Are Unsure of Relationships

Some teens are unsure of what to expect as they begin their first relationships, Jenkin said. If they haven't been taught to distinguish between healthy and non-healthy relationships, they may endure the abuse in an effort to please their abusers.

For others, like Rochelle, abuse is the norm. Perhaps they have witnessed abuse at home, or been victims themselves.

Aaron knows about being a victim. The 15-year-old wears the uniform of a teenager—basketball shoes and Walkman. But his quick smile dims when he speaks of the abuse in his own family.

> Dating violence is a reality for one of every three high school students.

"My stepdad used to beat us," Aaron said. "I had black eyes." He witnessed his mother being abused and often begged her to leave before it was too late. He wondered if it was something he did that caused his stepfather to fly into a rage.

Aaron vowed he would never abuse another person. But breaking the cycle of violence is not always simple. Research shows that violence perpetuates violence; children who have witnessed abuse are likely to become abusers or victims themselves.

"A lot of kids have myths about what makes up a good relationship," said Judy Kreiter, director of the Center Against Sexual Abuse. Each time she delivers a presentation in high schools, she's approached by students trapped in violence.

"Some of them are in crisis; a lot of them are in borderline situations and they don't know how to get out," Kreiter said.

Many are plagued by low self-esteem, feeling that no one else would ever want them. They may believe the abuser's promises that things will change, that the beatings or verbal abuse will end.

> The pressure to "fit in," combined with lack of dating experience, leads to teens' accepting violent relationships.

In short, Kreiter said, teens in abusive relationships face many of the same issues as adults.

In addition, however, many teens feel trapped in an abusive relationship by fear of losing popularity in their peer group, said Andrea Riteneur of the Preventing Abuse and Violence Program in Chandler schools.

Riteneur believes that the pressure to "fit in," combined with lack of dating experience, leads to teens' accepting violent relationships.

"Maybe you're more popular because you are dating a 'cool' person," Riteneur said.

Pressure Starts Earlier

Teenagers are facing pressures earlier and earlier, she said, while often unsure of expectations in a dating relationship. It is not uncommon for Riteneur to speak with 12- and 13-year-olds who consider themselves to be "exclusive" with a boyfriend or girlfriend.

Dating, or "going out," begins as early as junior high, agreed several Tempe, Arizona, teens interviewed at a local recreation center. And as teens get older, the pressure to be part of a couple increases and drives teens to stay in abusive situations.

Several said they have friends who have suffered physical and emotional abuse because they didn't know how to get out—in some cases because they didn't feel comfortable discussing it with their parents.

"In a lot of families, you don't talk about that (dating and sex)," said Perla, 17. "You go to your friends." Jan Sears, a counselor in the Glendale Union High School District, said parents should be open to honest conversation with their sons and daughters, encouraging them to discuss daily events and important topics. She suggested creating boundaries for the child early regarding issues such as setting an appropriate age to begin dating and deciding what curfew will be. She encourages group dating as an alternative to high-pressure one-on-one dates.

Sears believes it is up to parents, schools and an entire community to help teens discover themselves and create goals.

I Was Afraid to Leave My Abusive Boyfriend

Anonymous

Many teens get involved in abusive relationships as a result of low self-esteem. In the following essay, an anonymous teen describes her experiences with an abusive boyfriend and how her low sense of self-esteem made her endure his violent behavior. She writes that overwhelming feelings of worthlessness caused her to believe that she could never find a better boyfriend. In addition, her low self-image made her believe that she deserved her boyfriend's abusive treatment. After the relationship ended, the author eventually realized that she didn't have to put up with abuse in order to be loved.

The names in this story have been changed.

I was standing on the lunch line at my junior high school one day when I felt someone tug on my ponytail. When I turned around, a tall guy with short black hair was smiling slyly. I turned to my best friend and giggled. Then he did it again. I thought it was the cutest thing in the world. After we got our lunch, he sat at my table, but didn't say a word.

In French class, my friend Julie informed me that the guy with no vocal chords was named Danny, he was 15 and he wanted to go out with me. "I don't even know the guy," I said with a laugh. Julie smiled and said, "Look, just get to know him. If you don't like him, you can dump him."

He Made Me Feel Special

Danny followed me around to all my classes for the rest of the day but he didn't speak to me until after school, when he asked if he could walk me home. I told him he could. On the way, we stopped at the park and hung out for a while. We talked about our families, school, and music.

Danny had a sense of humor and made me laugh a lot. He seemed like a sweet guy. He was interested in everything I talked about and that made me feel special. I decided to go out with him. After all, what could I possibly lose?

I began spending time with Danny every day. We went to school together and hung out afterwards. He never failed to walk me all the way home. I felt like I could depend on him and I needed someone to depend on.

Safe in His Arms

Before meeting Danny, I was never happy with my life. My mother was forever putting down everything I did, making me feel worthless. I was yearning for someone to really love me and Danny became that person. I could talk to him about my problems at home, about how my mother and I never got along. He would hold me when I was feeling down and promise that whatever happened, he'd be there. Safe and secure, I clung to Danny. I thought I'd found my saviour. It took me a long time to find out I was wrong about him.

"I'm Going to Check on You"

One day, about three months into our relationship, I was wearing a bodysuit that I had just bought. When Danny saw me, he said, "You're *my* girl. Why do you want to wear that and show everyone what you have? Do you want to look like a slut?"

He handed me his hooded sweater and said, "Put this on and zipper it." He made me feel ashamed of how I was dressed, even though everyone was wearing bodysuits at the time.

I put on the sweater and zipped it partway up. Danny wasn't satisfied; he zipped it up to my neck. He looked me in the eyes and said, "I'm going to check on you, so don't even think about taking it off." I thought this was his way of showing affection. I thought it was so cute.

After that incident, Danny was constantly telling me what I could and couldn't do. I couldn't wear makeup, skirts or anything that he considered "slutty." I couldn't listen to R.E.M. because he thought they played "devil music." I couldn't go to the store. I couldn't even hang out with my two best friends, who I cherished. Danny started cutting all his classes so that he could "check on me" and make sure I was doing what he said.

At first, I didn't even notice how much Danny was controlling me. Love is blind and Danny was my first love. With him by my side, I was able to ignore my problems at home. As long as he was there, I was all right. In other words, I desperately needed him to cope with my own life.

His Girl, His Property

But soon my own life vanished. I needed him there so badly. I let him change the things about me that made me an individual. I was becoming a clone of Danny. I thought what he thought; I did what he did.

Danny justified giving me orders by making it clear that I was his property. "You're my girl," he kept telling me. And because I was his girl, I was supposed to listen to whatever he said. I didn't question this because I thought I'd be lost without him. I believed everything he told me, like "I'm the only guy who'll take your sh-t." All I needed was for him to hold me. As long as his arms were tightly around me, I got what I wanted out of the relationship.

I Did Whatever He Told Me

If I didn't do what he said, Danny would get angry—not just annoyed, but violently angry. As much as I hated admitting it, I was scared. I knew Danny had a short fuse and I didn't want to set it off. I was afraid of his temper but I was also afraid of losing him. So I obeyed him when he told me what to wear, to ignore all of my friends, and to stay home if he wasn't with me.

As far as my friends were concerned, I had dumped them for Danny. They thought I was just being a b—ch and I don't blame them. I didn't give them any reason not to hate me. I never told them how trapped I was feeling, how vulnerable. In a sick way, I wanted to be trapped because it made me feel secure.

One day, about a year after I started going out with Danny, he wanted me to walk to his house (which was about a mile and a half away). It was a freezing cold day when there were about four inches of snow on the ground and I said no. That was the first time I didn't do what he said.

The First Time I Said "No"

Danny gripped my arm, twisted it to where it was painful, and pulled me. We were standing outside in my neighborhood and some people were out shoveling their sidewalks. I said no again in a firm tone, but low enough so that no one else could hear me. He twisted my arm more. With his other hand, he grabbed some of my hair and yanked me forward. Tears were forming in my eyes. I realized that the more I resisted, the more hurt I'd get and the more the neighbors would notice, so I tramped through the snow to his house.

I figured that once we got there, he'd leave me alone since he'd gotten his way. I was wrong. I didn't even have a chance to get my coat off before he punched me. Danny hit me everywhere except my face (knowing that would leave visible marks). He did slap my face once though, which demeaned me completely. Then Danny shoved me into a chair and forced off my shoes.

> "I never said anything to anyone because I thought I deserved [the abuse]."

I began crying hysterically. The only person who cared for me (or so I believed) was treating me like I was nothing. Danny tossed my shoes on top of a cupboard where I couldn't get to them. "Shut the f—k up," he said. "Take your coat off, you ain't goin' nowhere." I just sat there sobbing.

After about an hour of giving me dirty looks, Danny started to feel bad and apologized for everything. "I just wanted to be with you," he said. We made up. A couple of hours later, he got me my shoes and I went home like nothing had happened.

Hitting Me Became an Everyday Thing

That type of incident became an everyday thing. I never said anything to anyone because I thought I deserved it. And I figured that having Danny hit me was simply the price I had to pay for having him hold me.

I became more and more isolated. Danny would only let me see my friends when he was there. Since he had no problem hitting me in public and I didn't want my friends to see that, I avoided them. I was too depressed to even talk to them about what was happening. I knew they would feel bad for me and try to get me to leave him. Although I wanted to, I was too frightened of having to cope with the dread of being alone.

Afraid of Him, Afraid to Leave Him

I did threaten to leave Danny a few times. His response was, "You can't get anyone else. Who would want you?" I believed him. I just accepted the low place I was in as my fate. This was all I thought I could ever amount to. I figured I would end up marrying him, dropping out of school and becoming a lonely, beaten-up housewife.

Things continued to get worse between us. One day, I was in the bathroom at Danny's house, combing my hair, getting ready to go out. I could hear him telling his sister and his cousin about a fight we had at a party. He had dragged me down a flight of stairs because I wanted to ask someone something. He had caused a commotion and a friend's parent had to drive me home so I could get away from him. Danny told his sister he had done what he did because I was a b—ch.

From the bathroom, I yelled out, "You're such a liar!"

Danny stormed in and pushed me hard enough to make me fall. I almost banged my skull on the bathtub. His sister started screaming, "I'm telling Mommy. I'm callin' the cops!" Then his mom came in with a bat and started swinging it at him. She turned to me and said, "Don't worry, I'm sending him to live with his father." Danny ran out.

I was so incredibly embarrassed. I wouldn't have cared if he killed me, but why did he have to do it in front of everyone? Danny's cousin was crying. She told me that he had grown up seeing his dad hit his mom. She begged me to leave him. "He'll never change," she said.

The cops arrived but Danny was nowhere in sight. His whole family was out in the hall and I had to walk past them to leave the house. They all stared at me pityingly. The police drove me home. This was the worst of all times Danny hurt me because his entire family and the cops were involved. Everyone knew what was going on. Everyone wanted to protect me from Danny, when I thought Danny was my only protection.

"I'll Change, I Promise"

For about four days after that, I tried to stay away from him. He would call me up and come to my house crying. I tried ignoring the phone calls and the doorbell ringing. I wanted badly to go out and see my friends, but when I did, Danny was there, a puppy-dog look on his face. "I'll change," he said. "I promise. I'm sorry." I gave in . . . again.

I still believed Danny loved me. He will change, I thought. But it was more like a hope. Sometimes hope just isn't enough. He never changed. He only got worse. I took his abusive treatment for another five months, until his mother finally sent him away to live with his father. At last, I was free.

I was lucky. I didn't have to break up with him. His mom took care of the dirty work. Looking back, I blame myself for what happened. I should've stopped the vicious cycle sooner. I guess I was stuck in a bottomless pit of self-pity. Not even a slap in the face could wake me up . . . and I mean that literally.

Never Again

For the first few months after Danny left, I didn't care what happened to me. I reunited with my friends but pretty much all we did was party. Then I met Greg. Neither of us was ready to jump into a committed relationship at first, so basically we became wonderful friends.

Greg made me realize that Danny wasn't the only person who could care for me. Greg not only cared, he supported me in a positive way. He insisted that I deserved a lot more than what I had. Greg somehow made me see that I had the power to accomplish anything. We started going out and have been together for two years now.

Writing this story has been the final healing phase for me. I am now a completely different person than I was when I was with Danny. Although it was a horrible experience, at least I learned a lesson from my relationship with him: The worst thing you can do to yourself is to depend completely on someone else. I will never do that again and I will never let anyone else control, abuse or hurt me in any way. I know now that you don't have to put up with that kind of treatment in order to be loved.

Love Shouldn't Hurt

Latonya Williams

If your boyfriend is hitting you or calling you names, he's not doing it out of love, writes Latonya Williams. She describes the abusive relationships of two of her friends, Jessica and Beverly, and the disappointment she felt when they chose to stay with their abusive boyfriends. According to Williams, if your boyfriend is hitting you, it is time to get out of the relationship, no matter how much he says he loves you. Williams is a writer for *Foster Care Youth United,* a magazine that covers topics pertinent to youths in foster care.

My friend Jessica has been going out with a guy named Kenyatta for three years. They are in love and she thinks he is the flyest guy out there. Every time I speak to her she's always saying, "Oh Tonya, look what Kenyatta brought me. Ain't this fly?"

Kenyatta treated her like a queen in the beginning of their relationship, buying her gifts and saying sweet things to her. I remember one time we were walking past this shoe store and Jessica said, "Yo, Tonya, those are the Tims my baby gonna get me for Christmas."

The Perfect Couple

For a long time I thought they were a perfect couple and I wanted a man just like Kenyatta. Who wouldn't want a man who kept his girl looking jiggy all the time and treated her like she was royalty?

Jessica could talk to Kenyatta about anything, even female matters, and he always understood. Not to mention the fact that Kenyatta's a dime-piece and all the girls wanted him. Things seemed to be perfect and I was mad happy for her.

At least that's what I thought until one day when I was in my lobby waiting for the elevator and Jessica came downstairs with a black eye. At first I thought she had beef, but when she told me Kenyatta did it I almost cried.

She tried to take up for him by saying "Nah, girl, it ain't nothing, he found out about that guy in the Pink Buildings, and you know, he got a temper. I rather have my boo care about me enough to hit me than not to give a damn at all."

Two weeks before I spotted her black eye, Jessica and I were on our way to the store and this guy in the Pink Buildings had tried to talk to her. They exchanged numbers, but she told him she had a man so they ended up just being friends. Obviously, Kenyatta didn't see it like that.

He's Always Sorry

When she tried to make excuses for Kenyatta's actions, I just looked at her and shook my head. I always thought Jessica had the sense to know when your man gives you a black eye, it's time to pick up and go.

The black eye incident happened in 1995 and Jessica is still with him. Jessica and I ain't all that cool now, because she moved and we grew farther apart. Now I only see her once in a while when she comes out to Brooklyn to visit her grandmother and to see Kenyatta.

While we were still cool I used to speak to Jessica a lot about

Kenyatta smacking her. I had only seen him hit her once, but she would tell me how he hit her on other occasions. I would tell her she should leave him because something must be wrong if he's hitting on her. The response I always seemed to get was, "I know, but Tonya you don't understand, that's my baby, I love him. He always says sorry when he hits me, and he be crying with me."

I can't imagine loving a guy who beats on me. When you have a man, your appearance and your spirit are supposed to be good. If your man is abusing you, you're gonna look toe up and you're gonna feel toe up (toe up means messed up), so that is not good for you.

> I always thought Jessica had the sense to know when your man gives you a black eye, it's time to pick up and go.

Jessica is not the only teen I know in an abusive relationship. I know other girls who put up with guys who abuse them. Not all of them are getting hit. Some girls I know are in relationships with guys who abuse them emotionally. These girls always seem to think their boyfriend is the best they can get. I don't know what it is that makes these girls love their boyfriends so much, all I know is they will do anything for them.

Trapped

For example, my homegirl Beverly, who's 17, is in a relationship with a 33-year-old man named Cortlandt. At first he seemed wonderful, a dime-piece, the whole nine. He would take Beverly anywhere she wanted to go and buy her anything she wanted. But no matter what Beverly wants to do, she can't do it if it doesn't involve him. She has to ask his permission to go to school because he thinks she should be home keeping him company.

Before she met him, Bev used to have a 4.0 average. She always kept her hair done and she and her grandmother had the best relationship. Now she lets herself go and neglects her school work. Cortlandt makes her feel like she's nothing when she leaves him. His demands have started problems between Bev and her family.

Beverly told me she stays with Cortlandt because she thinks that no one is gonna love her like he does.

No Man at All

I think Jessica and Bev are whipped. They're addicted to the affection that their man is giving them. They believe their man is God's gift, and figure so what if he stresses me out or beats on me—at least he loves me.

If your man is calling you names or if he hits you, he is not the right guy for you. If your man abuses you physically or emo-

---

Being a Friend to a Victim of Abuse

Most teens talk to other teens about their problems. If a friend tells you he or she is being victimized, here are some suggestions on how you can help.

- If you notice a friend is in an abuse relationship, don't ignore signs of abuse. Talk to your friend.
- Express your concerns. Tell your friend you're worried. Support, don't judge.
- Point out your friend's strengths—many people in abusive relationships are no longer capable of seeing their own abilities and gifts.
- Encourage them to confide in a trusted adult. Talk to a trusted adult if you believe the situation is getting worse. Offer to go with them for help.
- Never put yourself in a dangerous situation with the victim's partner. Don't be a mediator.
- Call the police if you witness an assault. Tell an adult—a school principal, parent, guidance counselor.

"Teen Dating Violence," available at www.ci.boulder.co.us/police/prevention/teen_dating.htm.

---

tionally, it's not because he loves you, it's because he's not man enough to channel his anger in a proper way. So he brings it home to wifey.

Even if you do have to make do without a man, that's better than being in a stress-filled relationship wondering why he shows "his love" in such a harsh way. You have to love yourself before you love your man.

I thank God I have never been in a relationship like Beverly's or Jessica's. One reason I think it hasn't happened to me is because my mother brought me up with enough love and self-confidence to know that I am worth loving the right way. I don't believe in settling for less than I deserve. I was raised by a mother who was always strong and never took sh-t from any man, and I can't imagine being in a relationship where I was abused.

When I meet a guy, I know whether he's immature or violent by the way he talks or presents himself. Once I come to the conclusion he will not be right for me, I usually keep him as an associate or nothing at all.

Get Out Quick

Yes, I know I sound like a pamphlet or some after-school special, but it's the truth. Saying, "Well, my man don't beat on me, he just smacks me around once or twice" is a messed up attitude, and you should learn how to love yourself before you decide to love someone else.

> I can't imagine loving a guy who beats on me.

To girls out there who are in relationships like my homegirls Jessica and Bev, get out quick before you find yourself laying in a hospital or worse. And to the ones who are not in those types of relationships, take my advice and never let your man make you feel lower than what you're worth. Peace out and stay strong.

Leaving an Abusive Relationship

Teen Advice Online

According to the counselors at Teen Advice Online, an organization that provides support for teenagers through a network of peers from around the globe, teens who are involved in abusive relationships need to find the strength to break free quickly. If your boyfriend is abusing you, he does not love you; no matter how much he apologizes for hitting you, he will not stop until you leave him.

Question:

I have been going out with my boyfriend for a year and half, but he drinks a lot and gets angry easy, and tends to take out his anger on me. He always pushes me or hits me or punches me or slaps me, but I take it, cause he's sorry. I really like him,and I know that if I dumped him, I would never get another boyfriend, cause I am guy shy and I have no self-confidence. People tell me to get away from him, but I can't. A few nights ago he broke a bottle over my head. Then one of my friends tackled him and beat him up. I now have an ugly scar. He called me the next day and told me he was sorry and that if I dumped him, he would kill himself. I feel the only way to get out of this is if I kill my-

Reprinted with permission from "Leave an Abusive Relationship," available at www.teenadviceonline.org/archive/a1077.html.

self. Help! I don't want to drag any cops or adults into this. I just want to die. Help me, please.

Anonymous Female, Age 15

Answers:

Kristi W.: I've been thinking about your help for a long time. You seem like such a sweet, innocent girl for such awful things to be happening to. Your boyfriend is bad. I know what I'm about to say is going to probably scare you . . . but, please . . . hear me out. You've already demonstrated to us that he has a history of violence. That's bad. He's already done many things to hurt you . . . so, first off . . . LEAVE HIM NOW!!! Whatever he may do to himself is NOT your concern. Get a restraining order. Tell people. If he's hurt you, he's going to hurt someone else. He might even KILL someone else. That's bad, too. Violent people don't tend to change easily.

You don't have to be a victim. We're here for you. The hardest part is getting the courage up to save yourself. It's all downhill from there, kiddo. I can't give you the courage to do it . . . I wish I could, because I would. But, I will be here for you long after this whole ordeal is over. I'll be your shoulder, I'll be your friend. And because you are such a beautiful person inside, no one in the whole world will care what you look like on the outside.

I believe in you. Please don't let him ruin your life. You deserve better than that. Many hugs and well wishes.

Manuela: Leave him, he's no good for you! You deserve someone who really loves you and cares for you. He has power over you, not love. If he loved you he would never hit you. You can have a wonderful life without him, he is abusing you. You can do a lot better. He gave you this low self esteem, if he didn't give you that you would have left him already. Don't feel guilty, it is not your fault he does this to himself he could

> Violent people don't tend to change easily.

change but he doesn't. Get out of there.

In a relationship there should be love that keeps everything together, not fear, guilt and anger. Dying is no option, you are a too beautiful person for that. Don't let him control you any longer but set yourself free, to find happiness.

What to Do If You Are Involved in an Abusive Relationship

Education Wife Assault, a Canadian organization dedicated to educating the public about spousal abuse, has developed the following advice for teens involved in abusive relationships.

If you are an abused teen you are not alone and you are not to blame. You cannot control his violence. But you can make yourself safer by:

- Calling the police if you have been assaulted.
- Telling someone and keeping a record of all incidents of violence.
- Talking to a trusted adult such as a parent, teacher, guidance counselor or school psychologist, and/or calling a community agency for advice.
- Considering ending the relationship as soon as possible. The violence may get worse.

"For Teens to Think About," available at www.womanabuseprevention.com/html/for_teens_to_think_about.html.

Deanna: Look, I know you think you really like him but you can't like anyone that hits you. People might tell you to get out of the relationship and those people are right, you have to for your own safety. If your boyfriend was so sorry then he wouldn't have hit you in the first place. He doesn't love you he just wants to control you for companionship. I think you should break up with him and get out of the relationship. Suggest that he sees someone professional and you probably should too because clearly he has caused you mental stress. Good luck!

Jillian: Sweetie, You *need* to tell somebody and get out of this relationship. Killing yourself is not a way out. People care about you. This guy doesn't. By staying with him, he feels he's in control. He knows your weak spots. I recently read a story about a girl that was in the same situation. She was afraid to get the cops involved because she was fearful that he'd kill her. Finally she told her parents and the cops did get involved, now he's in jail and she's safe.

> In my opinion having no boyfriend is better than having one that hurts you.

Your boyfriend is not sorry if he does it over and over again. Every extra day you stay in this relationship is hurting yourself more. First of all, there are millions of guys out there. Ones that will not hurt you. In my opinion having no boyfriend is better than having one that hurts you. Nobody has any right to harm you! I know you will find a guy like that.

Please tell your parents, or an adult you trust. They will really help you and help your boyfriend, he needs help. You are not ugly just because you will have a scar on your face! The scar might not even be very visible. I hope everything works out for you . . . remember: you are not the bad person.

Date Rape

Penny Ehrenkranz

Penny Ehrenkranz, a freelance writer, developed the following quizzes to help guys and girls recognize the warning signs of date rape. For girls, the higher the score on the first quiz, the more you have to learn about avoiding date rape. In addition to recognizing the danger of date rape, Ehrenkranz explains that girls should communicate openly with their boyfriends about limits and stick to them. If a rape does occur, Ehrenkranz explains that you should never blame yourself. No one ever asks to be raped. In the answers to the second quiz—for guys—Ehrenkranz clears up some common misconceptions about date rape. She also encourages guys to listen to their girlfriends and respect their limits. When a girls says, no, she means no.

Part I: A Quiz for Girls

Do you find yourself in a sexual wrestling match when you go out with guys? Have you gotten a "bad" reputation without doing anything to warrant it? Were you forced to go further than you wanted to? Take a few minutes with this quiz—it may help you recognize the warning signs of date rape.

1. Your boyfriend just took you to a fancy restaurant for dinner, then movies afterward. He paid for everything. You:

a. believe you owe him sex because he paid.

b. tell him "Thanks, I'll pay next time."

c. insist he bring you right home because your mom will ground you for a month if you're late.

2. Your parents aren't home this weekend. Your boyfriend wants to come over to do homework. You:

a. tell him "That's great—I'll be waiting for you."

b. tell him it's okay, but your girlfriend will be there too.

c. tell him you'd love to see him, but you can't have company while your folks aren't home.

> No woman or girl ever asked to be raped.

3. Yesterday you told your boyfriend you really care about him, but sex wouldn't be right. Tonight he says, "I know you want me; I can tell the way you're looking at me." You:

a. bat your eyelashes, snuggle closer and say, "maybe next time."

b. decide to avoid the issue and talk about other things.

c. say, "No—I said I'm not ready for a sexual relationship."

4. You think it's romantic to convey your feelings by special looks you share with your boyfriend. He thinks you want sex. You:

a. cry when he wrestles with you and say he should have known what you meant.

b. manage to avoid sex by making jokes.

c. have a serious talk with him about setting limits.

5. You've tried talking to your boyfriend about your limits. He refuses to listen. You:

a. allow him to have it his way because you can't change his mind.

b. talk to him again and hope he'll get it eventually.

c. get yourself a new boyfriend.

Score your answers to the test. Give yourself three points for each "a" answer; two points for each "b" answer; and one point for each "c" answer. The more points you tally, the harder you'll need to work to avoid becoming a victim.

Remember:

- Set limits and keep them.
- Communicate with your boyfriend.
- Assert yourself and stick with your decision.
- Listen to your boyfriend and set limits together—he has needs and wants also.
- Trust yourself.
- Be aware of how your boyfriend treats you—does he pinch you, tickle you, or hold you down?
- Don't let your boyfriend have all the power—share the decision-making.

If you're unable to avoid a date rape situation, seek counseling or call a rape crisis center immediately. Know that you're not to blame. No woman or girl ever asked to be raped.

For a listing of local rape crisis centers and hotlines, you can go to the Rape, Abuse & Incest National Network's Web site at http://www.rainn.org/. You can also call 1-800-230-PLAN for a local Planned Parenthood Health Center or go to the "Clinic Connections" section of this Web site to find the closest Planned Parenthood near you.

Part II: A Quiz for Guys

Hey, guys, do you really listen to your girlfriend when she's talking to you? Take the following True/False test and see how much you know about date rape.

1. Girls who hitchhike expect to trade sex for a ride.

    True   False

2. If you take a girl out to dinner and spend a lot of money, she should reward you with sex.

    True   False

3. Girls who wear sexy clothing are "asking for it."

    True   False

4. There has to be physical violence or a weapon in order for it to be rape.

　　　True　False

5. A girl can't be raped by her boyfriend.

　　　True　False

6. It's the girl's fault if she gets raped.

　　　True　False

7. Rape is just about a guy wanting sex.

　　　True　False

8. If a girl says no, she really means yes.

　　　True　False

How do you think you did? If you answered "false" to all the questions, you're a guy who's got all the right answers. If you didn't, you need to learn a few things about girls and rape.

Here are the real facts behind these false statements.

1. Girls who hitchhike do so for the same reason guys do. They need a ride someplace, but they're not offering to pay for that ride with sex.

2. Only spend money on a girl if you want to and can afford to, not because you want something from her. A better solution is to share the responsibility for a date including where to go and how much to spend. The girl should have some power too.

> When a girl says "no," believe it guys. She means, "No!"

3. Girls wear clothes which are in fashion. This doesn't mean they're trying to be "sexy." They just want to look good.

4. Date rape violence is commonly emotional. A guy who forces a girl makes her feel guilty, dirty, and ashamed. He doesn't have to beat her up or threaten her with a weapon to hurt her.

5. Rape occurs any time a guy forces a girl to have sex, even if they've had sex before!

6. No girl has ever "asked" to be raped. Whether she dresses sexy, has gotten drunk, accepted a ride from a guy, or flirts, she's not asking to be raped.

7. Rape isn't about sex. It isn't about fun. It's about power and control. Having sex with someone you love at the right time in your life is beautiful. Raping someone is not.

8. When a girl says "no," believe it guys. She means, "No!"

So, how did you do? Are you the kind of guy who knows what a girl wants? Do you know how to accept the limits she wants to put on a relationship? Are you willing to give up some of your control? You don't need to "prove" your manhood. Girls will know you're special by the way you treat them.

Remember:

- Most guys who say they're doing it aren't.
- Talk to your girlfriend about her limits.
- Be open and honest.
- Listen to your girlfriend.
- Trust her to tell you when she has reached her limits.
- Share the decision-making responsibilities.

Chapter 4

Avoiding Violence

Getting a Grip: Teens Talk About Anger

The Christophers

According to the Christophers, an interfaith religious organization, anger is a normal and healthy emotion that shouldn't be restricted or bottled up. The key to dealing with anger is to find a constructive way to let it out. Many teens find sports to be an effective outlet, while others find talking to a trusted friend, teacher, or family member to be a calming influence. If you have trouble getting your anger under control, do not be afraid to ask for professional help.

"Something that makes me really mad is when people underestimate me. They just write me off and don't take any time to really let me prove myself."

"I know I'm losing control when I start insulting others. One of my brothers has a learning difficulty, and once I got so mad I called him 'stupid.' I felt so bad about that."

"It seems I'm always getting angry and I don't know why. When I get mad, I usually take it out on my parents. Afterward I feel terrible. Sometimes I apologize. Sometimes I don't. Could you please help me figure out why I get mad so easily and how I can stop doing it?"

So You're Mad

You have probably felt like these teens: anger at something someone has done or said to you. And maybe you've tried to control your anger—and failed.

Young or old, everybody struggles with this very normal human emotion of anger. Sometimes anger is rooted in an experience or an unresolved situation from the past. You may think you have to protect yourself or your reputation. Whatever the cause—just like the teen above—the key is to "figure it out:" to understand what we are feeling and act for our own good—and the good of others.

What Is This Feeling Anyway?

You are angry. Your heart beats so fast you feel you could explode. Your mind races. And your first reaction is to punch a hole in the wall.

Anger is an intense feeling. It is hot displeasure. Hostility. Exasperation. It strikes most fiercely when things seem out of control. A body expresses anger through clenched fists, tightened stomachs and facial tension.

A psychologist who works with teens says, "Anger is a very normal process. You can't restrict anger; it's a message that something is wrong."

Anger can be triggered by personal hurt, insult, danger, frustration and disappointment. We might get mad because a brother or sister puts us down, because someone calls us names or bullies us, or because our parents just don't seem to pay attention.

> The key to handling anger is knowing why we are feeling what we are feeling—and dealing with it in an appropriate way.

Injustice can make us angry. We can be upset with the way friends treat someone who is "not part of the group" or who doesn't learn as fast or dress right. Maria says crime and violence in her neighborhood gets her very angry.

The key to handling anger is knowing why we are feeling what we are feeling—and dealing with it in an appropriate way. Anger itself is not a sin. But while anger may be justified, violence never is.

Doesn't Everyone Get Mad?

Of course, even Jesus got angry. He was upset with the money-changers in the temple, turning over their stands, saying His house was meant to be a "house of prayer" (Mark 11:17). On other occasions, He was angry with the scribes and Pharisees, some of the leaders of His day, because they were unjust.

But Jesus never got angry over a personal attack. And He never hurt or tried to hurt anyone. In fact, when Jesus was betrayed, arrested, put through a sham trial, mocked, tortured and finally killed, His reaction was love and forgiveness.

Does Anger "Hurt"?

It might help if we found this reminder on our cereal box or toothpaste tube: "Warning: Not dealing well with anger today can be harmful to your health—physically and emotionally."

Anger can make us do and say things that hurt ourselves and others. Anger can also make us feel ashamed. "I usually take out my anger on my little brother or sister. I really feel guilty," says Julie.

Sometimes we might get angry with people because they are different or just do not show enough respect. Others may get angry with us for the same reasons. Anger and prejudice can be linked.

If we always seem to get mad at or blame particular "types" of people for our difficulties, WE have a problem. WE need to step back when this type of anger strikes and remember that assaulting or provoking others can have serious consequences.

"Everybody gets angry sometimes. But you can learn to control anger," says Randy. "Give yourself time to cool off and think."

How Do I "Get a Grip"?

Maria says that her anger has driven her to hit her mother in the face. Another teen notes: "Most of the time, I keep my anger inside me. But when it's uncontrollable, I go inside my room and throw everything on the floor. I just explode. I go off."

Keeping your anger bottled up is not an answer—neither is beating up on yourself, others, or your room! What should you do?

Recognizing Violence Warning Signs in Others

The American Psychological Association (APA) has developed the following list of warning signs to help you determine if someone is at risk for violent behavior.

- loss of temper on a daily basis
- frequent physical fighting
- significant vandalism or property damage
- increase in use of drugs or alcohol
- increase in risk-taking behavior
- detailed plans to commit acts of violence
- announcing threats or plans for hurting others
- enjoying hurting animals
- carrying a weapon

"Warning Signs," available at www.helping.apa.org/warningsigns.

Start with a deep breath. Says Ken: "Try to calm yourself down. Count to three and take a deep breath. Relax. Then ask yourself questions like: Why am I angry? What's making me mad? What can I do about it? Slow down and give yourself some time to think." Take time to defuse rather than letting your fury escalate.

Arielle says: "I used to get really mad and throw stuff around. But now, I try to figure out what is really at the bottom of it. Lots of times I find it isn't even what started this anger."

Get physical. Randy finds sports a great way to work out his anger. "I'm in wrestling and football so I take it out on the mat or on the field," he says. "That way, I get rid of all that adrenaline and aggression."

Take a walk, work out, find a healthy outlet for your emotions and energy.

Let's talk. Talk problems out with friends, or with someone you trust: maybe a good friend, family member, school counselor, teacher or youth minister. But try not to hash it out with someone who will just add fuel to the fire and keep your anger raging.

Don't be afraid to ask for professional help if you have a serious or ongoing problem coping with your anger.

You should not have to put up with verbal or physical abuse either. If you need to confront someone you are angry with, do it, but not while you are upset. Avoid accusations. Keep your language calm and clear.

Standing up for yourself does not mean you should put down someone else. Again, ask for help if you need it.

Keep an "anger journal." Write down your feelings. This will help you to identify what makes you mad—and help you to resolve repeated conflicts. Or blow off steam by writing a letter to a person who is making you crazy, then rip it up!

The right recipe. Sometimes the answer for anger is the right blend of tolerance, respect and forgiveness. You're only human. So are the rest of us. Learn to accept and to forgive yourself and others.

> Everybody gets angry sometimes. But you can learn to control your anger.

Add a bit of humor. Carol Travis, author of *Anger: The Misunderstood Emotion,* recalls her own childhood anger and an afternoon of Charlie Chaplin films with her father. "There I learned that you cannot maintain a sullen mood when you are laughing out loud," she says.

Turn anger into positive action. Jennifer was upset about the way her high school friends and teachers didn't care about the environment. "They didn't recycle trash, and they didn't know how bad some of the products were they were using," she explains. Jennifer organized a recycling effort at her school. She also shared information about companies that use animals for testing or that caused ecological problems.

If there is a problem in your school or neighborhood, don't get mad, get moving—build up, don't tear down.

Pray. "If you know you have a problem controlling your anger, pray about it. Pray that God will work in your heart," says Liz.

Forgiveness, peace and love demand more courage than striking a blow ever could. If you trust God and try your best, you will meet your challenge.

Dealing with Bullying

KidsHealth.org

Whether you are being bullied or bullying others, there are many ways to avoid bullying behavior. For those who are being bullied, the best reaction is to walk away. Bullies thrive on the reaction of their victims and by ignoring the bully you will deprive them the reaction they are looking for. For those who feel the temptation to bully, talking with someone about the feelings behind the desire to bully someone—stress, anger, depression—can provide a constructive avenue of release. KidsHealth.org is one of the largest sites on the Internet providing doctor-approved health information about children and teens.

You and your friend have walked to school together for as long as you can remember. Lately, though, your friend doesn't laugh and joke like he used to and he seems distracted and jumpy. The other day he actually swore to you he was going to start carrying a weapon.

Maybe your friend is being bullied at school. It happens more than many people may think—about one out of ten teens is the victim of bullying at some point during childhood or adolescence. Maybe in comparison to school shootings like the one at Columbine High School [on April 20, 1999, Eric Harris and Dylan Klebold shot and killed twelve students and one teacher before turning their guns on themselves at Columbine High School in Littleton, Colorado], being bullied doesn't seem all that important. But if you've ever been bullied, you know that's not the truth. Bullying can change everything for you. . . .

What Is Bullying, Anyway?

Bullying is difficult to define because it can involve so many things. Any subject or person is fair game for someone who bullies. Maybe you've just gotten braces. At first, your friends teased you a little bit; you figured that would happen. There's one guy at school, though, who takes the teasing to a different level. His tone is mean and hurtful and it's all he ever mentions when you're around. Taunting or teasing like that is a form of bullying.

It doesn't have to be braces; a bully might target anything about you that is different. Maybe you're the tallest girl in your class or you're from an Orthodox Jewish home. Maybe you're Asian-American or you like to write poetry. And bullying can be done in countless ways: teasing, taunting, ethnic slurs, and sexual harassment are all forms of bullying. What they share is the power to upset or hurt the people who are being targeted.

Bullying can be physical, too. Maybe each time this guy sees you in the hall he intentionally walks into you and then blames you for being in his way. Or you might accidentally knock your books off your desk, only to have him accuse you of trying to trip him. What's even worse is that the bully isn't always just one person; sometimes a whole group singles you out and tries to taunt or hurt you. It can be really scary.

Why Are Some Teens Bullies?

Bullies can be tough to categorize. A bully may be outgoing and aggressive, the kind of person who gets her way through force or obvious teasing. On the other hand, a bully can appear pretty reserved on the surface, but may try to manipulate people in more subtle, deceptive ways, like anonymously starting a damaging rumor about someone just to see what happens.

Many bullies, though, share some common characteristics. They are generally focused on themselves and finding ways to seek pleasure. They are often insecure and therefore they may put other people down to make themselves feel more interesting or powerful. For them, it may be particularly difficult to see things from someone else's point of view. And some bullies act the way they do because they've been hurt by bullies in the past or because another person in their lives—like a parent or other family member—is abusing them in some way.

> One out of ten teens is the victim of bullying at some point during childhood or adolescence.

Standing Up for Yourself—or a Friend

Keep in mind that if you are concerned that you might be in physical danger, you must speak to an adult who can help you. No one wants to rat on someone, but your safety has to be your first priority.

Another thing to remember if you or a friend is being bullied is to avoid being alone. Try to remain part of a group by walking home at the same time as other teens or by always sticking close to friends or classmates, especially before and after school.

If you're being bullied and you're ready to stand up for yourself, there are some techniques you can try:

- Walk away and ignore the bully. It may seem like a coward's response, but it's not. Bullies thrive on the reaction they get and if you walk away, the message is that you just don't care. Sooner or later the bully will probably get bored with trying to bother you.
- Be confident; walk tall and hold your head high. Use your body language to show that you're not vulnerable.
- Try humor. If you can learn to laugh at yourself then you

won't give the bully the response he or she is looking for.

- However you choose to deal with a bully, don't use physical force (like kicking, hitting, or pushing). You can never be sure what the bully will do and violence never solves a problem, anyway.
- Talk about it. It may help to talk to a guidance counselor, teacher, or friend—anyone who can give you the support you need. Talking can be a good outlet for the fears and frustrations that can build when you're being bullied.

Resisting the Temptation to Be a Bully

It's common for teens to have to deal with a lot of difficult situations and emotions. If you're feeling stressed, angry, depressed, or frustrated, bullying someone else can be a quick escape—it takes the attention away from you and your problems. And if your friends respond by laughing and egging you on, it gives your self-esteem a little boost and reinforces your bullying behavior. Try to stop yourself right there and think about how your words and actions can hurt someone else. What may seem like innocent teasing to you can make a huge impact on another person's life.

If you find it hard to resist the temptation to be a bully, you might want to find someone to talk with. Talking can be a good way to release your feelings and frustrations and to look at a situation from a totally different perspective. For example, maybe hearing about how your older brother was bullied when he was in school would cause you to think a bit differently about the way you treat someone.

Getting Help

If your school has an antiviolence program, you might want to become involved in it. If not, maybe you'd like to start one. The National Crime Prevention Council has tips for organizing and starting such a program.

Other Web sites like Teen Central, Teens-Online, and Teen Sites, a Web directory for teens, offer info, resources, and areas where you can talk safely about these kinds of issues.

Finally, if your friend is being bullied, see if you can get him to talk to you about it. Then, maybe you can help your friend boost his self-confidence so he can react in a healthy, nonviolent way to the bullying. Try taking a stand by refusing to put up with bullies if you see them in action. If you hear someone taunting a classmate, for example, speak up and point out that this is no way to treat another person. You might be saving someone a lot of pain.

> Talking can be a good outlet for the fears and frustrations that can build when you're being bullied.

How to Avoid Violent Confrontations

KidsPeace

There are a number of ways that you can avoid violent confrontations, explain the counselors at KidsPeace. Avoiding violence begins with learning to value peace and learning to respect others. Treat people the way that you wish to be treated yourself and walk away from fights. It is important to not let your emotions get the best of you. KidsPeace is a help-line website written by teens for teens.

M aybe you feel like your world is a violent place. But you can do something every day to restore peace. To find your own sense of personal security. And to heal the wounds violence causes.

Here are some things to do. Though some take time, all offer immediate steps you can take to work out what's bothering you.

All are just suggestions. See what works for you!

• *Value Peace.* If you want peace, you have to value peace more than other things. Do you value it more than hate? More than revenge? Before you act, ask yourself "Am I helping keep peace or am I encouraging hate and retaliation?" If you desire peace, let peace guide your actions.

• *Respect Yourself By Respecting Others.* Violence occurs

when people don't value their neighbors or themselves. Get to know all kinds of people. Find out what's good about them.

Don't fall for blanket assumptions that encourage hate. Don't put up with racists jokes or put-downs. Treat people the way you'd want to be treated. You'll have more friends—and stay safer.

> If someone else is angry, you need to keep your cool to keep the peace.

• *Avoid Face-offs.* Violent people escalate trouble. They make snap decisions. They're quick to take offense.

So avoid face-offs. Walk away from fights, if you can. Realize that violent people are their own worst enemies. They're already upset. Don't add to the upset by facing off with a violent person, especially in front of a group of people.

• *Keep Talk From Escalating Into Violence.* It's human to want to share your troubles with those close to you. And if you or someone you love has been a victim, you'll want to talk about it with your friends and family.

But leave justice to the proper authorities. And remember, violent people create violence for themselves. They live violent lives and die violent deaths. If you don't want to die that way, don't live that way.

• *Chill.* Don't let your emotions make you violent. If someone else is angry, you need to keep your cool to keep the peace. When you let them get you angry and upset, you give them power over the situation. Keep your cool.

• *Get Involved Elsewhere.* If you live in a violent area, take advantage of any safe places—after-school programs, teen clubs, church activities. Anything to keep you off the streets and away from the gangs. Protect your peace of mind where people care about your life and your problems.

• *Ask For A Change.* The stress of living with violence can be wearing of your peace of mind. Maybe you need a temporary change. Could you visit relatives somewhere else for a time? Go to camp? Get a part-time job in another neighborhood? Get a wider slice of life. You'll discover there is more to the world than violence.

• *Get A Peaceful Point Of View.* If you want to live in peace, talk to peaceful people. Get their opinions. Pose the tough questions to your teachers, youth counselors, religious leaders. Talk to a veteran about violence. They'll probably be able to tell you how horrible and senseless violence can be.

Just Walk Away

Diana Zborovsky

According to Diana Zborovsky, today's teens are under more stress than ever before. This stress often leads to violent outbursts. If you are faced with a stressful situation and feel that you may snap, Zborovsky advises that you just walk away. It may be difficult to do, but it is the best solution. Spend some time by yourself, Zborovsky explains, and think about why you are angry. Chances are that you will realize you got worked up for nothing. Zborovsky also recommends participating in activities that will take your mind off your anger, like exercise, music, and painting. Zborovsky is a writer for *Teenvoice.com,* an online magazine written by teens for teens.

These days, teenagers have a lot to deal with: school, friends, family, etc. Teenagers of today are under more stress then those of any generation before. The heavy amounts of stress that we face may lead to unusually high outbursts of anger from today's youth. Unfortunately, this anger is quite often expressed violently. We have seen examples of this quite often in the news recently. Unfortunately, teenagers just do not know how to channel their anger. So, I am here to help you.

If you are in a situation where you know you are going to

Reprinted with permission from "Controlling Your Anger," by Diana Zborovsky. Article available at www.teenvoice.com/Magnifique/Health/Anger/index.html.

get very mad at someone and maybe even snap, just walk away. I know that sounds like it might be hard to do, but don't worry, it will work. Just walk away without saying anything. I would recommend that you go sit by yourself and think about why you are mad and then realize why, in most cases, there was no reason to get so worked up. Sometimes, all you have to do is take a few deep breaths. This will ease your tension when you become stressed. Another method to removing anger that works well is to sing the words to your favorite songs when you become angry and feel as though you are about to explode. Not only will this take your mind off the anger, the song might actually make you feel happy.

> If you are in a situation where you know you are going to get very mad at someone and maybe even snap, just walk away.

Some people like to run or exercise when they become angry. Exercising diverts their attention from their anger. Basically you can do anything that will help you take your mind off your feelings. Paint, read, watch movies, or play your guitar. Do anything that works for you.

Don't Argue with Your Parents

A common pastime of teenagers is fighting with parents. Personally, I never understood this, because I believe that no matter how temperamental or strict your parents may be, they are YOUR parents and they love you no matter what. Do not argue with them! Instead, go to your room and try to put yourself in their shoes. In 30 years you will be glad that you weren't too mean to them. Try to enjoy your time with them before you go off to college. If you have a problem with them, instead of standing their and yelling at them, leave for a while, think about your reasons for being angry and then go back and talk to them like a reasonable adult. It will fix the problem and show your parents that you are actually maturing.

One final point I would like to make is that VIOLENCE SOLVES NOTHING! I cannot stress this more! The only thing it will do for you is get you in trouble. It will not change anything. Do not hit anyone; do not cut anyone; and *please* do not try to seriously injure or kill anyone. It is never worth it!

Creating Safer Schools

Marilyn Sherman

Stemming the tide of school violence will take a com-bined effort on the part of teachers, students, parents, law enforcement officers, and the community, explains *Current Health* contributor Marilyn Sherman. In order to ensure a safe learning environment for students, school officials need to install metal detectors to keep weapons out of schools and implement zero-tolerance policies for drug use, bullying, and weapons possession. In addition, stu-dents must learn to walk away from confrontations and ex-plore other ways of settling disputes.

One beautiful day in October on the Purdue University cam-pus in Indiana, an 18-year-old freshman strolled into his dorm. Blaming his RA (resident assistant, or dorm counselor) for the trouble he had gotten into for cocaine possession, the boy pulled out a gun and shot the older student dead.

This situation shows signs of the same troubling violence that has infected high schools across the nation. Not just inner-city schools, but all kinds of schools—suburban and rural as well as urban—have been affected. Every year, there are nearly 3 mil-lion incidents of theft or violent crime in or near schools.

Have weapons become as much an accessory in a backpack

as a calculator? More than 41 percent of teenagers surveyed by Children's Institute International said they don't feel safe at school. More than 46 percent said violence was increasing at their school. Gangs, guns, media violence—along with poverty, drugs, and disintegrating families—all contribute to the threat of violence in schools.

It's a Team Effort

Combating the complex problem of school violence must be a team effort. Students, the school, the community, parents, law enforcers, courts, and religious leaders all need to work together to make schools safe.

Many schools have effective safe-school plans. And a key to many successful schools' plans is peer mediation or mediation by outside volunteers. Working with trained mediators, both sides in a dispute hear each other out and work toward a solution that both can accept.

> More than 41 percent of teenagers surveyed by Children's Institute International said they don't feel safe at school.

Safe-school plans also may include these measures:

- metal detectors to prevent weapons from being carried into school
- zero-tolerance rules for drug use, bullying, and weapons possession
- graffiti crackdown to erase gang symbols
- security guards to head off trouble
- locker supervision to keep drugs and weapons out of the school
- transparent backpacks to keep weapons out of the school

Across the country, the wave of violence is meeting with a wall of resistance. Students who violate violence-free codes are being expelled more frequently. In 16 states, students patrol and report crimes through the Youth Crime Watch program.

A school action plan is only part of the answer. Each individual in the school has to be part of the solution on a personal level. Even if you're not directly involved in a confrontation, you're still involved. Responsibility rests with the majority not to allow bullying to go on at school. On a personal level, you can show your strength by helping to prevent violence in these ways:

- *Know you can be tough by backing down.* Sometimes the smartest thing to do is to walk away from a confrontation. It can take more guts—and be cooler—than to give in to anger and fight. Police say most youth homicides result from someone not backing down from a fight.
- *Understand ways of dealing with confrontation.* There are times to avoid it, times to use reason or humor, and times to assert yourself. Have an appropriate range of reactions, not an on/off switch.
- *Listen.* Use active listening skills, even repeating aloud the other person's viewpoint to make sure you understand it.
- *Know what your body language says.* Just a look can be interpreted as a stare down and may start a major fight.
- *Be assertive when it's safe and appropriate.* Effective responses can be saying "Don't do that!" or "Stop it!" and walking away. Anger and combativeness only escalate conflict.
- *Get tough on yourself.* Be firm about being responsible for your own behavior. Keep your anger in check. When there're no refs to put you in the penalty box, do your own self-policing. Sit out, take deep breaths, and count to ten when you feel yourself becoming confrontational. Keep a lid on your own tendencies to violence. You'll thank yourself for it.
- *Avoid bad situations.* Do what it takes, whether it's sticking with a supportive group, walking away, or taking a different route home.
- *Use peer mediation.* Look to the program at your school, or request one if your school doesn't have it. Use a go between to talk out and resolve a conflict so that both sides win.
- *Go for extracurricular activities.* Make sure your school has

them for all interests, and get involved. School activities, along with work experiences, are safe alternatives to gangs and can boost your self-respect.

If you have a problem with violence—either your own or someone else's—get help. See a teacher or other adult you trust. A small insult or negative look can blow up into a violent crisis. If somebody at your school gives you a bad look or hits you with a put-down, what do you do—make a joke, tell him to quit, or punch him? Depending on where you are and whom you're with, your choice could mean the difference between a falling-out and a fatality.

Schools around the country are working to be safe havens for students (see sidebar below). Safe schools put the squeeze on guns, drugs, and gangs—and squeeze out violence. But your school has to be able to count on you to come through a conflict with a cool head.

Securing Safe Schools

Safety is at the top of the priority list at the Metropolitan School District of Lawrence Township in Indianapolis, Indiana. "Safe schools are everyone's business. We all have to work together to resolve common issues," states Assistant Superintendent Duane Hodgin. Teachers, students, parents, and the community—all are cooperating partners working for safe schools in the district.

In 1994, motivated by rising violence around the country, the district enacted a safe-schools plan for grades K through 12. With key elements of prevention, intervention, education, and involvement of everyone, the plan helps the district be prepared.

Sometimes the smartest thing to do is to walk away from a confrontation.

A district with a diverse population and economic extremes, Lawrence Township was the first in Indiana to have a board-adopted safe-schools policy. It was also first to have a crisis of incidents such as the taking of student hostages or student unrest.

An important part of the safe-school plan is having "police support officers" on the high school premises but outside the buildings. The trained, off-duty police officers are available by radio if they are needed inside. "While their role is to help, serve, and prevent, their visible presence contributes to security," says Dr. Hodgin. Since the program began, vandalism has been almost wiped out, and there have been no guns on campus, he noted.

> Safe schools put the squeeze on guns, drugs, and gangs— and squeeze out violence.

While the school district acknowledges that there are gangs in the area, it doesn't cave in to gang behavior at school. There are little ways, such as banning hats in school, and major ways, such as working with an area gang task force.

What also counts is education for both teachers and students. Drug education and education about bullying are two prime topics. And the school trains students as peer mediators so that when disagreements arise, those involved can refer themselves to peer conflict management programs.

Other safe-school practices include having a closed campus with visitor badges, locked doors, sign-in procedures, security cameras, mirrors, handheld radios, and an emergency communications network. The school takes surveys and conducts safety audits.

What this adds up to is a feeling of security. In a recent survey, most district high school students said they wanted law and order, and they overwhelmingly approved of the police support officers. Ninety percent reported feeling safe. Dr. Hodgin notes, "From analyzing the data, we know we're making a difference."

Organizations and Websites

The editors have compiled the following list of organizations concerned with the issues debated in this book. The descriptions are derived from materials provided by the organizations. All have publications or information available for interested readers. The list was compiled on the date of publication of the present volume; the information provided here may change. Be aware that many organizations take several weeks or longer to respond to inquiries, so allow as much time as possible.

American Academy of Child and Adolescent Psychiatry (AACAP)

3615 Wisconsin Ave. NW, Washington, DC 20016-3007
(202) 966-7300 • fax: (202) 966-2891
website: www.aacap.org

AACAP is the leading national professional medical association committed to treating the 7 to 12 million American youth suffering from mental, behavioral, and developmental disorders. The AACAP publishes the monthly *Journal of the American Academy of Child and Adolescent Psychiatry,* as well as the book *Your Adolescent,* a guide for navigating the difficult issues that arise during adolescence.

American Civil Liberties Union (ACLU)

125 Broad St., 18th Floor, New York, NY 10004
(212) 549-2500 • fax: (212) 549-2646
website: www.aclu.org

The ACLU is a national organization that works to defend Americans' civil rights as guaranteed by the U.S. Constitution. It supports students' rights to privacy and free expression and opposes the implementation of zero-tolerance policies in schools. ACLU publications include the monthly *Civil Liberties Alert* and the quarterly newsletter *Civil Liberties*.

Children's Defense Fund (CDF)
25 E St. NW, Washington, DC 20001
(800) CDF-1200 • (202) 628-8787
e-mail: cdfinfo@childrensdefense.org
website: www.childrensdefense.org

The Children's Defense Fund advocates policies and programs to improve the lives of children and teens in America. CDF's Safe Start program works to prevent the spread of violence and guns in schools. The fund publishes a monthly newsletter, *CDF Reports*, as well as online news and reports such as "Children in the States: 1998 Data" and "How to Reduce Teen Violence."

Handgun Control
1225 Eye St. NW, Suite 1100, Washington, DC 20005
(202) 898-0792 • fax: (202) 371-9615
website: www.handguncontrol.org

Handgun Control is a citizens' lobby working for the federal regulation of the manufacture, sale, and civilian possession of handguns and automatic weapons. The lobby publishes the quarterly newsletter *Progress Report* and the book *Guns Don't Die—People Do*.

National Institute of Justice (NIJ)
National Criminal Justice Reference Service (NCJRS)
PO Box 6000 Rockville, MD 20849-6000

(800) 851-3420 • (301) 519-5500

e-mail: askncjrs@ncjrs.org • website: www.ncjrs.org

A component of the Office of Justice Programs of the U.S. Department of Justice, the NIJ supports research on crime, criminal behavior, and crime prevention. Among the numerous reports it publishes and distributes are "Serious and Violent Juvenile Offenders," "Adolescent Violence: A View from the Street," and "Partnerships to Prevent Youth Violence."

National Rifle Association of America (NRA)
11250 Waples Mill Rd., Fairfax, VA 22030

(703) 267-1000 • fax: (703) 267-3989

website: http://www.nra.org

With nearly 3 million members, the NRA is America's largest organization of gun owners. The NRA believes that gun control laws violate the U.S. Constitution and do nothing to reduce crime. It publishes the monthly magazines *American Rifleman, American Hunter,* and *Insights,* the NRA's magazine for junior members.

National School Safety Center (NSSC)
4165 Thousand Oaks Blvd., Suite 290, Westlake Village, CA 91362

(805) 373-9977 • fax: (805) 373-9277

e-mail: june@nssc1.org • website: www.nssc1.org

NSSC is a research organization that studies school crime and violence. The center believes that teacher training is an effective means of reducing these problems. Its publications include the book *Gangs in Schools: Breaking Up Is Hard to Do* and the *School Safety Update* newsletter.

Parent Project
2848 Longhorn St., Ontario, CA 91761
(800) 372-8886 • fax: (909) 923-7372
e-mail: training@parentproject.com
website: www.parentproject.com

The Parent Project is an award-winning model for school and community programs serving high-risk families. Focusing on the most destructive of adolescent behaviors, the Parent Project's training program, *A Parent's Guide to Changing Destructive Adolescent Behavior*, offers no-nonsense solutions to the serious problems parents face raising children in today's world.

Partners Against Violence Network (PAVNET) Online
(301) 504-5462
e-mail: jgladsto@nalusda.gov • website: www.pavnet.org

PAVNET Online is a virtual library of information about violence and youth-at-risk, representing data from seven different Federal agencies. Its programs promote the prevention of youth violence through education as well as through sports and recreation. Among PAVNET's curricula publications are *Creative Conflict Solving for Kids* and *Escalating Violence: The Impact of Peers*. The monthly *PAVNET Online* newsletter is also available.

People Against Rape (PAR)
PO Box 5876, Naperville, IL 60567
(800) 877-7252 • fax: (630) 717-0391
e-mail: peptalk@insnet.com • website: www.empowerme.com

People Against Rape primarily seeks to help teens and children avoid becoming the victims of sexual assault and rape by providing instruction in the basic principles of self-defense. Publications include the books *Defend: Preventing Date Rape and Other Sexual Assaults* and *Sexual Assault: How to Defend Yourself.*

Youth Crime Watch of America (YCWA)
9300 S. Dadeland Blvd., Suite 100, Miami, FL 33156
(305) 670-2409 • fax: (305) 670-3805
e-mail: ycwa@ycwa.org • website: www.ycwa.org

YCWA is dedicated to establishing Youth Crime Watch programs across the United States. It strives to give youths the tools and guidance necessary to actively reduce crime and drug use in their schools and communities. YCWA publications include a variety of resources on beginning new Youth Crime Watch programs as well as the book *Talking to Youth About Crime Prevention,* the *Community Based Youth Crime Watch Program Handbook,* and the motivational video *A Call for Young Heroes.*

Websites

KidsHealth
www.kidshealth.org

KidsHealth is one of the largest sites on the Internet providing doctor-approved health information about children from before birth through adolescence. This website provides teens with information on violence, bullying, and school safety.

Teen Advice Online (TAO)
www.teenadviceonline.org

TAO's teen counselors from around the world offer advice for teens on violence, dating, family, school, and substance abuse. Teens can submit questions to the counselors or read about similar problems in the archives.

Teen Voice

www.teenvoice.com

Teen Voice is an online magazine that provides teens with a forum for the expression of their ideas and comprehensive coverage of events and news in a way that makes clear and relevant connections among the experience of teens and the larger community.

Teenwire

www.teenwire.org

This website was created by Planned Parenthood to provide teens with information about sexuality and dating issues. The site offers an online teen magazine, searchable archives, a question-and-answer forum, and informative articles about teen issues.

Bibliography

Books

Sibylle Artz   *Sex, Power, and the Violent School Girl.*
                             Toronto: Trifolium Books, 1998.

Marian Betancourt   *What to Do When Love Turns Violent:*
                             A Practical Resource for Women in
                             Abusive Relationships. New York:
                             Harper Perennial, 1997.

Richard L. Curwin   *As Tough as Necessary: Countering*
and Allen N. Mendler   *Violence, Aggression, and Hostility in*
                             Our Schools. Alexandria, VA:
                             Association for Supervision and
                             Curriculum Development, 1997.

John Devine   *Maximum Security: The Culture of*
                             Violence in Inner-City Schools. Chicago:
                             University of Chicago Press, 1996.

Charles Patrick   *Kids Who Kill.* New York: Avon, 1995.
Ewing

Suellen Fried and   *Bullies and Victims: Helping Your Child*
Paula Fried   *Survive the Schoolyard Battlefield.* New
                             York: M. Evans, 1998.

Irwin A. Hyman and   *Dangerous Schools: What We Can Do*
Pamela A. Snook   *About the Physical and Emotional*

Abuse of Our Children. San Francisco: Jossey-Bass, 1999.

David W. Johnson   *Reducing School Violence Through*
and Roger T. Johnson *Conflict Resolution.* Alexandria, VA: Association for Supervision and Curriculum Development, 1995.

Bob Larsen   *Extreme Evil: Kids Killing Kids.* Nashville, TN: Thomas Nelson, 1999.

Richard Lawrence   *School Crime and Juvenile Justice.* New York: Oxford University Press, 1997.

Barrie Levy   *In Love and in Danger: A Teen's Guide to Breaking Free of Abusive Relationships.* Seattle: Seal Press, 1998.

Maryann Miller   *Coping with Weapons and Violence in School and on Your Street.* New York: Rosen, 1999.

Joy D. Osofsky, ed. *Children in a Violent Society.* New York: Guilford, 1998.

Kelly A. Zinna   *After Columbine: A Schoolplace Violence Prevention Manual.* New York: Spectra, 1999.

Periodicals

Peter Applebome   "Two Words Behind the Massacre," *New York Times,* May 2, 1999.

Susan Bailey   "Adolescents Who Murder," *Journal of Adolescence,* February 1996.

Jonah Blank | "The Kid No One Noticed," *U.S. News & World Report,* October 12, 1998.

Timothy C. Brennan Jr. | "Uneasy Days for Schools," *Newsweek,* June 29, 1998.

Nancy D. Brenner et al. | "Recent Trends in Violence-Related Behaviors Among High School Students in the United States," *Journal of the American Medical Association,* August 4, 1999. Available from 515 N. State St., Chicago, IL 60610.

Gail Lumet Buckley | "The Gun Cult," *America,* October 19, 1996.

Kathryn Casey | "When Children Rape," *Ladies' Home Journal,* June 1995.

Geoffrey Cowley | "Why Children Turn Violent," *Newsweek,* April 6, 1998.

Carey Goldberg | "For Those Who Dress Differently, an Increase in Being Viewed as Abnormal," *New York Times,* May 1, 1999.

Andrew Goldstein | "Ready and Waiting," *Time,* April 24, 2000.

Blair Golson and Ralph Frammolino | "Schools Finding Fewer Guns, U.S. Says," *Los Angeles Times,* August 11, 1999.

John Hundley | "In the Line of Fire: Youth, Guns, and Violence in Urban America," *Journal of Adolescence,* December 1996.

Irwin A. Hyman and Pamela A. Snook	"Dangerous Schools and What You Can Do About Them," *Phi Delta Kappan,* March 2000.
Andrew Jacobs	"Violent Rites," *New York Times Upfront,* April 24, 2000.
Jean Hanff Korelitz	"How Well Can We Ever Know Our Kids?" *Newsweek,* March 6, 2000.
Jodie Morse	"Looking for Trouble," *Time,* April 24, 2000.
Sasha Nemecek	"Forestalling Violence," *Scientific American,* September 1998.
Cheryl K. Olson	"Making Schools Safe," *Parents,* November 1997.
Ralph R. Reiland	"Would Stephen King Be Jailed?" *Humanist,* January/February 2000.
Russell J. Skiba and Reece L. Peterson	"The Dark Side of Zero Tolerance: Can Punishment Lead to Safe Schools?" *Phi Delta Kappan,* January 1999.
Patrick Welsh	"The Price of Protection," *U.S. News & World Report,* May 3, 1999.

Index